SUFFERING IN SILENCE

The Journey to Surviving Pulpit Depression

Foreword by Dr. Jeffery D. Robinson

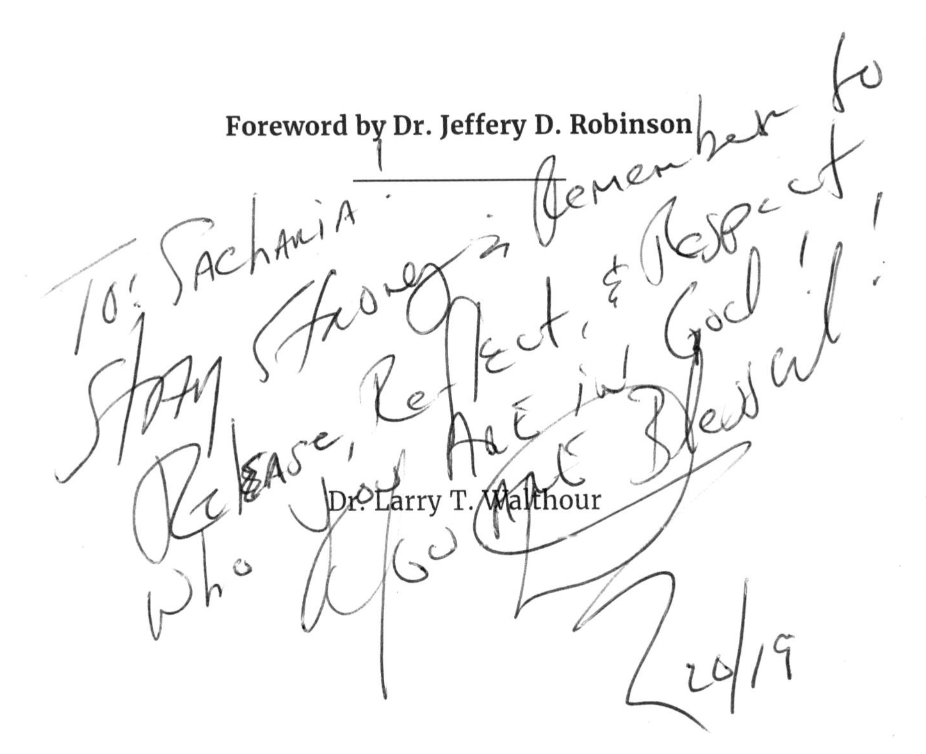

Dr. Larry T. Walthour

Suffering In Silence: The Journey to Surviving Pulpit Depression

ISBN: 978-1-64316-738-1

Published by LiveWealth Publishing
Printed in USA by CreateSpace

To contact Dr. Walthour:

Shiloh Baptist Church
740 W. Locust Street
York, Pennsylvania 17401
Phone: 717.854.2547
Email: sbcmainoffice@sbcyork.org

DEDICATION

This writing is dedicated to all who are fighting, have fought, overcome, and survived depression. I am eternally grateful for the chance to share a voice for those who often don't have one. This writing is my testimony of how God healed me from the spirit of depression through the power of prayer, praise, and persistence. I pray these words are a source of liberation for those who are still bound by depression.

Notice I said God has "healed" me from depression and not that He has "made me whole" from depression. There is a huge difference between the two. When God heals you from something, it can return to attack you. When God makes you whole from something, it cannot and will not ever attack you again. In 2008 I was "healed" from depression; I am yet to be made whole.

Each day I fight to stay in a place of deliverance from the spirit of depression. This fight is a constant reminder of where I am and how far I have come in this journey. Although the fight is sometimes difficult, I am encouraged by God's awesome power. It is through His Spirit and by His power that I have been able to overcome the spirit of depression.

To my Lord and Savior Jesus Christ, I am eternally grateful for the gift of salvation and the favor of His everlasting love. It is because of Him and by His grace that I am able to share the words of this testimony.

To my wife Michelle, thank you for your words. Each day I use them as a motivating reminder to never go back to that dark place called depression. To Lachelle, Shanika, Olvins, Janelle and Kalai, thank you for being true to who you are and to who you are becoming. You are truly blessed and favored by God and the lessons that I've learned and taken from you have been priceless.

To my mother, Ora L. Walthour, father, Larry T. Walthour, Sr., Dr. Janice Walthour (Ma' Janice), mother-in-law Marie Innocent (mum), my sister, Lavencia Yvette Jean, and brothers, Fred and Leonard Barnes, thank you for never settling and always striving for bigger, better, bolder, and brighter.

To Sister Tawana Guthrie-Russell and Lakeshia Guthrie, thank you for being there over the years. To the Wyartt (Nelson and Lorine), Jones' (Frank and Pamelisa), Lemon (Vernon and Sheryl) (Arnold and Kim), and Walker (Frank and Alice) (Betty) families; thank you for your prayers and for providing me a place of habitat in your homes like Mary and Martha of Bethany provided for the Christ.

To Rev. Duane Thomas (my brother from another mother) and Dr. Jeffery Robinson (for the powerful foreword), thank you for your rich, relevant, and rewarding words of spiritual truth and insight on the Divine Text. This project could not have been birthed without your words of wisdom in my most difficult hours. I am ever grateful for your friendship and partnership in ministry.

To the memory of the Late Dr. Mack King Carter and the many other preachers, pastors, and prognosticators of Calvary who have sown into my life throughout the years. Thank you for allowing God to use you as instruments of inspirational insight during my times of distress, despair, and deliverance.

To Deacon Anna Williams and Sis. Christine Beverly who provided editorial insight while serving as an extra set of eyes in the review and editing process of this writing. Thank you for your time, tenacity, and temperament in ensuring this writing reflects the highest level of Kingdom excellence.

To the St. Andrew Baptist Church in Miami, Florida, thank you for 27 years of serving, sowing, and sharing in the ministry of God's

Word. I am grateful for the new chapter God is fulfilling in your lives as He leads you to higher heights and deeper depths in Him.

To the officers (diaconate), clergy, servant leaders, members, ministry team, and administrative staff of the Shiloh Baptist Church of York, Pennsylvania where I serve as Senior Pastor. Thank you for being a **"Church Determined to Know Christ in Excellence."** I am thankful to God for the opportunity to lead, love, and labor with such a special group of Kingdomites.

Thank you for pushing me to excel in the worship of the Messiah, the work of the ministry, and in writing of this manuscript. Your excellence in ministry at all levels of operation is second to none – you do God proud!!

TABLE OF CONTENTS

FOREWORD

Dr. Larry T. Walthour has been entrusted with a tremendous gift, and I count myself privileged to call him friend and brother. A series of providential events caused our paths to cross over a decade ago, and from that day up to this present time his life and ministry has made an indelible imprint upon me. His anointing expository preaching and teaching has become for me a tributary of renewal and revival in times of personal drought. Moreover, I am fully convinced that this book will make a similar impact upon the lives of every reader. Whether you are a pastor, leader, or layman, this book offers a unique perspective and practical guideline that will equip you to better approach and handle the epidemic of depression.

This book is special to me as I have dealt with extended seasons of despair while attempting to successfully facilitate ministry during my pastorate. There were times that I sank so low that the idea of rising again seemed totally improbable. Were it not for the mercies of God that sustained me through those seasons of difficulty, I would not have made it. God graciously provided for me by connecting me to vital resources that infused life into my soul. This book is destined to become a tool to assist ministers and laypersons alike navigate feelings of heaviness while offering hope to others.

To those of you who may be experiencing the "dark night of the soul", please keep reading. It is my sincere prayer that this publication will become a divine instrument in the hand of God to lift you out of the valley of despair. It is a great relief to know that you don't have to suffer in silence! Just like many of the great titans of our faith, you can overcome pulpit depression. Your breakthrough is pages away!

Dr. Jeffery Robinson, Senior Pastor
Mt. Carmel Baptist Church, Daytona, Beach

PREFACE

This book is birthed out of pain that comes from the suffering of the soul. Suffering is not something with which we are unfamiliar. Everyone born in this world has had (or will have to) to deal with some form of suffering. Suffering is the process of experiencing intense physical, spiritual, emotional or mental pain, distress, and/or hardship. Suffering can be internal, external, or eternal. Whatever the state, the effects from suffering can be devastating.

Although any form of suffering can be difficult, suffering in silence is deadly and destructive. My suffering in silence is the story behind my story. My suffering in silence is my story of choice. My suffering in silence is my story of silence. Silence is often described as the complete absence of sound. In my suffering, I chose to be silent – absent of sound, soundless. I take full responsibility for my silence because you don't overcome depression by blaming others for being depressed. While I do not believe anyone chooses to be depressed; I do believe we choose how to deal with depression. My method of choice was silence. At the time, I did not see it as a choice of right or wrong but as a choice of survival.

Looking back, I thought surviving depression was predicated upon silence. I chose silence because I didn't know where to go or who I could trust. In the movie industry, they say "Silence is Golden." When fighting depression, silence is anything but golden – it is grim. While talking about depression might sound easy, it's not. It is very difficult to talk about depression when you are depressed.

Depression is a quiet storm within the soul and the absence of hope. Depression is the constant feeling of distress, dejection, despair, and despondency. In my season of depression, I felt hopeless and silence was a means to an end. It is amazing how depression can affect your thinking. It makes you think differently than you would under normal circumstances. Depression makes you think that not addressing a situation causes it goes away. This is a defeated and dangerous way of thinking that cannot be further from the truth.

Satan is the ultimate deceiver behind depression. When you are deceived into thinking silence is the way out of depression, you are destined to remain in a state of self-destructive suffering. I came across the following quote by Mitch Clark that I believe puts depression in its proper perspective:

"People think depression is sadness. People think depression is crying. People think depression is dressing in black. But people are wrong. Depression is the constant feeling of being numb. Being numb to emotions, being numb to life. You wake up in the morning just to go back to bed again. Days aren't really days, they are just annoying obstacles that need to be faced. When you're depressed, you grasp on to anything that can get you through the day. Even in a strange way you fall in love with your depression because you think it's all you have."

Depression is more than emotional distress, mental trauma, extreme sadness, and/or lethargy. I believe Depression is a spirit. Throughout this writing, I will often refer to depression as the "spirit of depression." If depression is a spirit, then you must have a spiritual strategy to overcome it. I believe the only way to be completely delivered from the spirit of depression is through the power of God's Word. In addition, God may use various means and methods to help you overcome depression. I am convinced that God uses pastors, social workers, mental health counselors, therapists, intercessors, clinicians, and many other professionals to help bring you to a place of healing and wholeness. Ultimately, it is the power of God's Word that frees you from the spirit of depression.

Let the journey to freedom from depression begin...

INTRODUCTION

Depression is the dark night of the soul that oppresses the mind and spirit. It is an internal conflict with eternal and external consequences. It is a dark place that leaves you drained, dry, and in despair. Depression is a house of destruction whose residents experience a slow and painful death. When you are depressed, hope is replaced with despair, joy is replaced with sorrow, and passion gives way to pain. Each moment in time seems like an eternity – seconds seem like minutes; minutes seem like hours; hours seem like days; days seem like weeks; weeks seem like months; months seem like years; years seem like decades; decades seem like centuries; and centuries seem like millenniums. Depression mocks time.

My journey towards depression began in 1995. After the passing of my pastor, I had been confirmed as his successor and new Senior-Pastor of the St. Andrew Missionary Baptist Church. Afterwards, a *small* group of individuals contacted the District Association and State Convention to challenge the legitimacy of the vote. After reviewing their complaint, the District decided to schedule a second special call meeting.

At the meeting, the minutes from the first meeting were read, questioned, and adopted for the record. Upon hearing the reading of the minutes, the Moderator and other officials spoke for the record that the minutes proved the legitimacy of the first vote. Even still, the "loyal opposition" sought grounds for a challenge – my heart sank because these were people I had worked with for the past seven years. After a rather tense and heated conversation from the floor, the Moderator closed the discussion, asked me to step outside, and proceeded to call for the second vote.

Since I was pastor-elect, my name was the only name under consideration for what would be an up or down vote. If voted up, I would be reconfirmed as Senior Pastor. If voted down, the church would organize a search committee to find a new pastor. In the event of a search committee, an interim pastor would be called and I would need to submit my resume with other viable candidates. Either way, my future with the church would be decided that evening. When the dust settled, God once again confirmed my assignment. The first vote was an 87%-10% affirmation with 3% abstaining. The second vote was a 93%-5% affirmation with 2% abstaining. When God is for you, He is for you.

Going home that evening, I had a different view of the people I had served with in ministry for the past seven years. The seeds of anger and resentment had been sown in my spirit that evening. As much as I tried, I could not make sense out of what had transpired. It was difficult not to allow my disappointment and anger in a few people to become a root of bitterness towards the entire church. Now that I was the pastor, I had to love the entire membership. That included those who supported me and those who did not. I did not know it at the time, but that night changed the trajectory of my life and ministry. I had no idea that I had just begun a journey towards depression.

My assignment as senior pastor was joyful and painful. It was joyful because I had an opportunity to equip God's people for the work of the ministry. It was painful because some of those I had served with for the past seven years had become a "loyal opposition" for no apparent reason. I had served with them, shared with them, and sacrificed for them. I did not admit it then, but I was deeply wounded.

Wounds may heal, but the scars obtained from those wounds last forever. In my wounded state, those scars would become the backdrop of depression. As one who has fought depression personally and professionally, I am a living witness that God is able! I can relate to your struggle and will be the first to admit that overcoming depression is not easy. For five (5) years, the spirit of depression had built a spiritual stronghold in my life. During those years, life became a living nightmare as I suffered in silence. But if you looked at my life from the outside, you would not have known how much I was suffering on the inside.

In many ways, I was like a functioning alcoholic. Unlike the alcoholic who drinks until his life literally falls apart, the functional alcoholic appear absolutely normal. Looking at him, you would not know he were an alcoholic or had a problem with alcoholism. I was a pastor who was a "functioning depressant" – under severe depression while acting and appearing normal.

During those five (5) years, the spirit of depression invaded my life to the extent that I struggled to wake up, get up, or even leave home. Soon, my clothing began to mirror my inner conflict. Instead of wearing clothes that reflected color and vibrancy, I (without realizing it) wore clothes that were dark, bland, or mundane. I had no life and to be truthful, I had no desire for living. I wanted out of this misery but didn't know who to trust. Had I succumbed to my inner conflicts and taken matters into my own hands, I would not be writing these words today. In my season of depression, life was a living hell that rotated on a perpetual cycle of hurt, humiliation, and hopelessness.

I am writing this book for two reasons. First, to help those fighting depression. Listen to me very carefully. If you are fighting depression, you are under a spiritual attack. Do not confuse your feelings of loneliness, abandonment, shame, and anger with being crazy, insane, or delusional. I know your pain - you are not crazy or losing your mind. The attack on your life is very real and has great consequences. Like me, you might be suffering in silence without any glimmer of hope. Silence is not your friend; it's the enemy. Silence does not erase or eradicate depression; it enhances it. Overcoming depression requires opening your mouth and speaking life into your situation through your testimony. You must talk about your experience and share your story with others.

The second reason is to offer hope. Hal Lindsey is credited for stating the following: "*Man can live about forty days without food, about three days without water, about eight minutes without air, but only for one second without hope.*" Without hope, you cannot overcome the spirit of depression. Despair is the opposite of hope and in the words of President Barack Obama, you must have the "audacity of hope." Hope keeps you from giving up and tells you depression will pass. Hope says that by reading this book, you are a survivor because you have weathered the tempestuous storms of depression. You are a survivor because you have withstood the stormy seas of personal despair. You are a survivor because you did not wilt under pressure.

My friend, you are a survivor so don't throw in the towel!! Never forget that God has not brought you this far to fail, fall, or falter. You are here for a purpose so don't allow depression to discourage you. Discouragement is the slippery slope from which you fall into the raging waters of depression. Depression destroys your spirit and leaves you feeling hurt, helpless, and hopeless.

Don't give up! Keep the faith and fight to tell your story. Your story must be heard and only you can tell it. No one can tell or share your story like you. Don't allow the spirit of depression to silence your voice!! Your voice is powerful because in your mouth is the power of life and death. In your mouth is the power of the tongue. Open your mouth, lift your voice beyond your despair, and SPEAK LIFE INTO YOUR SITUATION!!!!

“The one sitting on the throne said, "see, I am making all things new!" he said, "write this: 'these words are trustworthy and true.”
- Revelation 21:5

Chapter One:

A New Beginning

***

I will never forget Miami, Florida, March 26, 1995. At age 37, my pastor at the time (the late Rev. James C. Ferguson, Jr.) had transitioned to be with the Lord and I had been confirmed as his successor in pastoral ministry. At age 27, I was the third pastor in the history of the church and was filled with excitement. For the past seven years, the St. Andrew Missionary Baptist Church (aka “the Drew”) had been my church home. In addition to serving as his youth minister, I was also his ministry assistant and was at his home when he transitioned.

This was my first pastoral assignment and I was blessed with some good people. With a congregation of approximately 200 adults (including children and youth), the church had a reputation of being a very spirited and lively congregation who appreciated the Word. I was fortunate to serve under a pastor who was serious about study and believed in preparation, presentation, and proclamation. In the pulpit, he often emphasized the preaching experience by the creed: "PREACH or PERISH!"

Sunday services were filled with loving prayer, lively praise, and liberated preaching. As youth minister, I was taught the importance of scriptural study, sermon preparation, and sound preaching. Moving forward, I knew life at St. Andrew would take some getting used to. I had some large shoes to fill; the problem was that we didn't wear the same shoe size. Like most transitions, my transition from youth minister to senior pastor was not easy.

I was trained to watch pastors in the pulpit because they set the tone for worship. Everything a pastor does or does not do in the pulpit during worship has a subtle impact on the worship experience. As I grew into my new assignment as senior-pastor, I developed a new perspective of ministry. The work of the ministry was not as easy as it had seemed before. When you are the pastor, the work of the ministry affects you differently. I came to realize that in pastoral ministry, depression attacks when you try to resolve things that are beyond your control. If you do not come to a point where you learn to trust God with the results, depression will be tapping you on the shoulder. Since the church belongs to God, He adds the measure of increase (Acts 2:47). My pastoral assignment was to pray, prepare, and preach. I have learned to pray for God to send laborers into His harvest (Matthew 9:38), prepare the membership for the work of the ministry (Ephesians 4:11-12), and preach the gospel of Jesus Christ (Romans 10:17).

One lesson my 30 plus years of pastoral ministry has taught me is that people are in your life for reasons and seasons. I have seen this time and time again in my pastoral ministry. Never get discouraged or depressed when people decide to leave. God just might be making room for others. This happened in the life of Christ and it will happen to you. Consider the following passage from St. John 6:66-69:

[66] *From that time many of His disciples went back, and walked no more with Him.*

[67] *Then said Jesus unto the twelve, Will ye also go away?*

[68] *Then Simon Peter answered him, Lord, to whom shall we go? thou hast the words of eternal life.*

[69] *And we believe and are sure that thou art that Christ, the Son of the living God.*

Seasons and reasons are a part of life. Don't give in to despair, depression, or discouragement when people leave! The absence of people does not mean the absence of God. God is always present! If people walked away from Jesus, they will walk away from you. People must fulfill their purpose for being with you and when they do, God will either move them or move you.

Many of Jesus' followers left because they could not control His destiny. They had witnessed Jesus feed 5000 men (besides women and children) with five loaves of bread and two fish and they wanted to make Him king by force! (St. John 6:15) Jesus' experience teach us a valuable lesson: sometimes followers want you to fulfill their dreams and ambitions. It's like a parent living precariously through their child or children. Although this was my first pastoral assignment, but I was in for some very tough lessons.

Tough Lessons

Learning lessons are not always easy – especially tough ones. Not long after accepting my new assignment, I learned three valuable lessons. Some would say that these events were a prelude to my future season of depression. While this may or may not be true (I really can't say), they were valuable lessons just the same:

Lesson One: Trust. In this new season, I had to trust God with the results. Like in the life of Christ, many left when I became Senior Pastor. Although this was a painful lesson, it was one I needed to learn early. I didn't understand it at the time, but God was shifting the ministry and those who left, had to leave. Had they stayed, they would not have followed my leadership or submitted *to* my pastoral authority. God assigned me to be their partner, not their pastor. As their partner, I was to labor with them – not lead them. Pastoring and partnering with people are two different things. Whereas pastoring requires leadership and partnering requires labor, both require love.

In my finite understanding, I didn't see what God was doing. God was pruning the church and teaching me how to love people by releasing them. Because I was focusing on those who left, I was missing out on the move of God. When you focus more on people than purpose, you miss a whole lot. To see God's plan for your life, you must focus on His purpose. God's purpose for my life during this time was to prune. By pruning the church, God showed me not everyone within the fold was of the flock.

Many who left were good people but they were not good for me at this stage of ministry. Though they were in the fold, they were not a part of the flock God was giving me. It was very painful to see the musician, drummer, youth directress, mission director, and others walk away. In my mind, I was still wounded from what happened before. First, it was the vote and now it was the visionary. I felt rejected as a person, a preacher, and a pastor. Yet still, God was trying to show me these were not my sheep.

In St. John 10:27, Jesus says *"My sheep know my voice and a stranger they will not follow."* Because those who left were not my sheep, they could not hear my voice or follow my leadership. I was a stranger to them. The sheep must know the shepherd's scent and the sound of his voice. Since these people were not my sheep, they could not hear my voice or adopt my spirit. I had to release them because holding on would have been sinful and selfish. Although painful, their leaving was purposeful – not personal. Because I considered them close friends, releasing them was difficult. When it is time for you to release others, trust God enough to let them go.

Lesson Two: Thanksgiving. I was thankful God was using those who stayed to become a new "Joshua Generation" of leaders and members within the congregation. People who were once on the sidelines were stepping up to serve in ministry. Not only were these members getting involved, they were making contributions. Consequently, I was able to see the giftedness God had placed in this ministry. Had those who left stayed, the remnant would not have had the opportunity to develop their gifts and serve at a higher level.

After the *exodus*, I analyzed and assessed the remnant who remained. Surprisingly, the remnant was a greater resource for ministry than those who left. God uses remnants to revive, restore, renew, and rebuild. By doing so, He moves and works in ways that defy logic. I have found that God blesses just as much (if not more) through subtraction as He does addition. In retrospect, I was not aware God was adding through subtraction. Never count God out of your situation. If God is pruning your life or your ministry, celebrate His subtraction in your life!

Lesson Three: Transition. As God transitioned the church, I noticed there was a subgroup in the ministry that stayed because they were more *connected* to the building than they were *committed* to the vision. There will always be those who love the past more than the future. People love buildings because the time they have invested over the years is too much to walk away from. Although this group stayed, I was not their pastor -- *yet*. As a matter of fact, this group hardly ever called me "Pastor." Instead, they called me "Rev.", "Reverend", "Preacher", or some other term of ecclesiastical endearment. I may have been the *pastor* for the church, but I was not *yet* the pastor of this group. I soon realized their initial support had nothing to do with me because they did not yet have my heart for the ministry. Call it sentimental, but they supported me because I was connected to something they loved—the building. Their investment in the building over the years had far outweighed any value they had for me or any other new pastor. It took me a while, but I finally figured this out.

Confidants, Constituents, and Comrades

My sister's name is Yvette Jean and we are five years and one day apart. My mother went into labor on my fifth birthday and my sister was born a few hours after midnight. Growing up in Jacksonville, Florida, we developed a close relationship. Even though we had sibling rivalries, we were close. My sister and I could fight among ourselves, but God help the person who dared bother either of us. Growing up, if someone other than an adult tried breaking up a fight, we would put our fight on pause, handle them and then resume our fight! Even to this day, we are still like that – don't mess with my little sister! Who knew that my little sister would one day become what I would consider a confidant.

Bishop T.D. Jakes taught a powerful lesson where he talks about *confidants*, *constituents*, and *comrades*. In this teaching, he identifies three groups of people in our lives and their various differences. He warns that if we are not careful, we will place people in one group when they should be in another.

At this point, I wish to paraphrase what Bishop Jakes' says about *confidants*, *constituents*, and *comrades*. First, he explains that ***confidants*** are people who are in your life for you. These people love you unconditionally and are with you no matter what. These are what you would call the ride or die folk who you can't get rid of. It doesn't matter whether you are right or wrong, up or down, in trouble, in despair, in distress, or in depression – they are with you for the long haul. You can tell them anything and not be ashamed because they will never judge you, condemn you, change on you, or abandon you.

Confidants are for you even when they know things about you that you are afraid others will find out.

He further states that a confidant's sole purpose is to help you reach your destiny and fulfill your Kingdom purpose (although they may not share your specific goals, beliefs, or ambitions). A confidant will challenge, confront, and chastise you all the while sharpening your iron with honesty, honor, and humility. Without confidants, you will never become who God has called you to be.

Confidants are rare. If you find 2 or 3 confidants in your lifetime you are blessed!

Secondly, he states that ***constituents*** are people who are for what you are for but NOT for you. You and your constituents are for the same things. Although they are not for you or even into you, they will walk with you, talk with you, and work with you as long as you are for the same things. Since constituents are not for you, they can meet someone who furthers their agenda and leave you for them. Constituents are easily mistaken for confidants because you share the same mission and causes. If you stop being for the same things, constituents may change and/or become indifferent towards you. Constituents are temporary people who move in and out of your life and you must not confuse them with confidants. Never mistake the temporary for what is permanent.

Finally, he explains that ***comrades*** are those people who are against what you are against. Unlike confidants (who are for you), and constituents (who are for what you are for), you and your comrades are against the same things. Comrades are not for you but will work with you to fight a greater enemy. Although they may be on your team, they are not your teammate. Comrades are with you until a purpose is fulfilled or a victory is won. These individuals live by the creed, "the enemy of my enemy is my friend." Comrades are like scaffolding on a building. They enter your life to fulfill a purpose and when that purpose is complete, they (like scaffolding) are removed. Since these people are not for you, don't become depressed when they are removed. Remember, scaffolding is meant to be removed but the building remains.

Bishop Jakes' pointed, powerful, and profound insight helps us put our circles of influence into proper perspective. My fight with depression taught me how to have the right people around me and how to put those around me in their proper place. If you are going to survive depression, you must know your confidants, constituents, and comrades.

Renewal

In Revelation 21:5, John declares that God makes all things new. God is Faithful and only He can restore your situation without rewriting your story. During one of the lowest points in my life, God heard my silence and inclined His ear to my cries. I can relate to the words of David as found in Psalm 116:2,

> [2]*Because He hath inclined (got close) His ear unto me, therefore will I call upon Him as long as I live.*

With God, our silence is an unspoken language. Even when we are silent, God hears the supplication of the heart. David uses the word incline to suggest God comes close to hear what we have to say. In my bout with depression, God came close. He not only heard me but He listened to what I had to say through silence. God inclined His ear to my inner pain and allowed this book to be birthed in the process. Through His grace, I have been renewed, revived, and restored.

God wants to restore you through the process of renewal. Notice I wrote "the process" and not "a process" (more will be said about process later). God takes you through a specific step-by-step process by which He makes you better than before. God used depression to make me into someone stronger, wiser, and better. Trust me when I say, God makes all things new! God used a bitter place to make me a better person. In His hands, depression was a tool to make me better. Contextually, the word *new* suggests something that has already been in existence but is now seen, experienced, or received for the first time. When God renews you, it is as if He has created you for the first time. In your new and exciting season, I decree that you are going to be better than before! You are going to look new, think new, act new, walk new, talk new, and be new! This is your new season of life and freedom from depression!

A Divine Declaration: *Lord, I decree and declare through Your Name that my new beginning in You will give me a new season of life and freedom from depression!*

"I had fainted unless i had believed to see the goodness of the lord in the land of the living" - psalm 27:13

Chapter Two:

Valleys and Crossroads: Surviving in the Low Places

***

I officially began my assignment as Senior Pastor of the St. Andrew Missionary Baptist Church on March 26, 1995. The early years of my pastorate had been quite fulfilling and things progressed quite well. Besides the pains learned from those earlier lessons, I had a relatively good pastoral experience. In the early years, we experienced a wonderful season of favor, fellowship, and family. I was thankful that God was at work in the life of the congregation and church. At the time, I had no idea that my season of peace was the proverbial "calm before the storm."

The Valley Experience

It came from nowhere. I hit a very low point in my life and tried to make sense of where I was. I had preached many sermons about how life's mountaintop encounters are followed by valley experiences. My study of Scripture allowed me to preach on this subject through hermeneutical interpretation and sermonic homily on numerous occasions. Although I knew this, I did not see it coming. I was unprepared in an unfamiliar place. God had been so good to me on the mountaintop that I had forgot about the pending valley. I was like Peter at the Mount of Transfiguration - so happy to be on the mountain that I just wanted to stay there.

My first seven years of pastoring was promising and brought great progress. As a church, we had become armed and dangerous in "Spiritual Warfare" through the teachings of my dear friend and brother, Rev. Dr. Michael Johnson of Pensacola, Florida. In spite of the great blessings we experienced as a ministry, what started out with such promise and purpose had collapsed into something very painful. I knew mountaintop moments were followed by valley experiences and I should have seen this coming.

I was in the eighth year of pastorate and in a lonesome valley. Valley experiences are always accompanied by isolation and loneliness. For some reason, my pastoral assignment had become stagnate and without growth. Something was very wrong with this picture. As I surveyed my spiritual terrain, my unfamiliar territory made even less sense. I was taught that we reap what we sow; reaping this type of spiritual frustration did not add up because as far as I could tell, I had not sown this. I had spent years sowing good seed (time, talent, and treasure) into the lives of others.

On the surface, everything was going just right. Sunday worship was good and I was preaching the Gospel of Jesus Christ as I had been called and trained to do. Each week, God allowed me to preach and teach a Rhema word that was relative to the needs of people. As far as I could tell, I was faithfully obeying God's direction while leading His people into greener pastures.

However, somewhere between preaching and teaching there was a lack of reaching. The ministry was at a point where new members and converts were not joining and several faithful supporters decided to relocate or go to other ministries. This was even more painful because I had invested personal time and resources to help them get back on their feet during their time of personal loss or crisis. It seemed as if I was a good enough pastor to help them get back on their feet, but not good enough to cover them once they started walking. When asked about why they were leaving, I received answers like, "I just feel the need to go deeper in the Word" (a personal insult if you ask me) or "I believe my season here is complete", or (my personal favorite) "It's not you Pastor, I love your preaching and teaching, but some of those members..." Feel free to complete the sentence on that last one. I had not realized it, but I was wading in the waters of depression. I experienced this when I first became pastor and the pain was no less devastating now as it was then.

To make matters worse, I was angry with God and my anger had become a root of bitterness. I felt as if God was being unfair in my situation and could not see why He allowed my ministry to falter while others flourished. I was giving my all as a pastor and observing the 'green grass' of these other ministries frustrated me more. Furthermore, colleagues who gave less to their ministries were receiving much more in return. While my anger was hidden from others it was obvious to me and God. Each week I slipped further and further into depression without really knowing I was depressed in the first place. The spirit of depression had subtly attacked my faith and crippled my hope in God.

Attacked and Crippled

My faith had been attacked and I was crippled. It is difficult to confront or combat depression when you don't know the symptoms. The spirit of depression manifests itself through a variety of ways. These ways include: changes in behavior and/or sleep patterns, loss of interest in regular activities, extreme sadness, low energy, weight loss/gain, fatigue, feelings of little or no value, irritability, lack of focus, and suicidal thoughts. Like many who fight depression, I was slowly slipping into its murky waters. My complaint against God was like that of Jeremiah (Jeremiah 20:7):

> [7] *O LORD, thou hast deceived me, and I was deceived; thou art stronger than I, and hast prevailed: I am in derision daily, every one mocketh me.* [8] *For since I spake, I cried out, I cried violence and spoil; because the word of the LORD was made a reproach unto me, and a derision, daily.*

Like the Prophet Jeremiah, I felt as if God had deceived me into pulpit ministry and He was to blame for this. Had I known it was going to be like this, I would not have accepted God's call to the pulpit! Depression is especially dangerous for those in pulpit ministry. As a pastor, I am responsible for watching over the souls of others – a very difficult task when your own soul is in turmoil! For me, depression produced feelings of anger, anxiety, and abandonment. In my anger I became anxious, felt abandoned by God, and silently blamed Him for what my life had become. I was at a place where the last thing I wanted to do was to talk to God (pray), thank God (praise), or talk about God (preach) [I will discuss my dilemma with prayer and praise later]. In my depression, I was becoming someone I didn't know. Depression changes you for the worst. If you are struggling with depression, use every ounce of strength you have to live in this moment. In this moment, don't give up on yourself. In this moment, don't give up on others. In this moment, don't give up on God! My friend, embrace and enjoy this moment without giving up!

Since I no longer wanted to preach, my preaching was empty, effortless, and emotionless. My passion for preaching was all but gone as I was preaching on the fumes of my faith and not on the fuel of God's Word. Preaching the traditional "Sunday Sermon" and teaching the weekly "Bible Study" did not change the fact that God's Word was hollow and empty for me. There is nothing like preaching and teaching from a Bible in which you have lost faith. The spirit of depression had choked my spiritual lifeline and I struggled to survive. Depression drained the life out of me as God's Living Word became a lifeless Word to me. The Holy Text from which I preached had become mere letters, words, numbers, and sentences on a page. In short, the Bible was ink on paper.

I was called to preach God's Word. However, preaching had become a chore that was reduced to duty without desire. I preached because it was my duty to preach; not because I desired to preach. Every person God calls to preach must have a desire for preaching. Without desire, preaching is an empty exegesis of an ancient text. Through desire, preaching springs to life with fresh purpose, passion, and power! In my season of depression, I had lost my passion and become stale, stagnate, and stuck in the valley.

Surviving in the Valley

The pulpit is a place of elevation. Although it is an elevated place, it is not a platform. There is a reason why this unique place of elevation is called a pulpit and not a platform. Those who are privileged enough to stand behind it do so to proclaim the Gospel of Jesus Christ as a means to "pull" people from the "pits" of life. Hence the name – pulpit. Looking back, I am amazed to see how God uses us during our lowest moments to stand so high.

Pulpit depression is a different type of depression. It is depression on steroids. The spirit of depression uses depression as a weapon to attack your faith and overwhelm your spirit. This spirit uses depression as a means to an end. The end result of depression is valley experiences. It takes great faith to travel through life's valleys. In Psalm 23:4, David describes the valley as being a place filled with the shadow of death and evil. Consider the words of David:

> *4Yea, though I walk through the valley of the <u>shadow</u> of death, I will fear no evil: for thou art with me; thy rod and thy staff they comfort me.*

These words have comforted countless amounts of people in times of despair, discouragement, and discontent. A valley is a low place surrounded by hills and mountains. In our valleys, we are surrounded by what seems to be insurmountable challenges. However, some lessons can only be learned in the valley. Talking about the valley is one thing, but testifying about the valley is another. Testifying about the valley is to have lived through and experienced it. I have learned that valleys serve two purposes.

The first is to bring us to a place where we can exercise our faith and evaluate our focus. "Is this my fault?" "Am I to blame for this?" "Had I done something to warrant this in my life?" "Am I reaping what I have sown in the lives of others?" "Where is God and what is He trying to show me through this?" These questions originate from the shadows of death around us. In spite of these shadows, we must keep the faith and stay focused. The spirit of depression is an evil force that casts many shadows and lurks in every valley. A shadow is created when a source of light is blocked. God is Light, therefore a shadow is produced when something comes between you and God.

When depression came between God and me, it caused a dark shadow in my life. The shadow of depression is an illusion of darkness – not darkness itself. Darkness is the absence of light and cannot exist in and of itself. Light exists *with* or *without* darkness but darkness can only exist without light. Without the absence of light, darkness cannot exist. Your shadow is a dark area; it is not darkness. If you are fighting depression, God is the Light that sees you through dark shadows. The darkness you feel is the shadow of depression that comes between you and God. Shadows might be intimidating, but they cannot harm or hurt you. No one has ever been attacked or destroyed by a shadow.

The second purpose of the valley is to experience God. When depression leaves you in the valley, God meets you there. Before becoming king, David shepherded his father's sheep and clearly understood the relationship between the shepherd, the sheep, the rod, and the staff. To the shepherd, the rod and staff represented protection and was used to defend the flock from attack. To the sheep, that same rod and staff represented correction and comfort. When the sheep strayed, the stick (rod) was used to guide the sheep and correct its direction. When the sheep were in trouble, the hook (staff) was used to rescue it from danger and provide comfort. Your life is not over because of depression. There is life before, during, and after depression. Surviving depression means making it through the low places. Sadly, fear and the lack of faith prevents millions of people from surviving depression. Through fear and the lack of faith, the spirit of depression causes you to see things in the shadows that are not really there.

Shades, Shadows, and Silhouettes

Shades, shadows, and silhouettes are not the same. In fact, they are drastically different. *Shade* is not something we fear – it is something we seek. We seek shade to find refuge from the sun or heat. When I resided in South Florida, it would get immensely hot and on those hot, humid, or warm sunny days, people would often walk, run, sit, or even play in the shade. In a place like South Florida, *shade* is pleasant, soothing, and enjoyable. Some days it would be so hot, you sought shade from wherever you could find it – a tree, a building, a house, etc. In the light of the sun, these objects cast enormous shadows that provided much needed shade. Because I recognized the source of the shadow, I was never afraid of its shade.

A *shadow* refers to an area of darkness created when a source of light is blocked. Shade and shadows can be confusing. While shade is associated with light, shadows are associated with darkness. We are not afraid of shade because we know where it is coming from. We fear shadows because they suggest something is mysterious, unidentifiable, dangerous, or threatening. It is in not knowing the source of the object where a *shadow* has power to deceive and produce fear through darkness. In the dark, objects that were highly visible and recognizable during the day are made to appear very strange and scary at night.

A *silhouette* is a **dark shape** and/or **outline** of something or someone that is visible against a lighter background. Like shade, a silhouette is identifiable. During the day, the silhouette of a tree on the ground provides the shade we need to escape the sun's heat. However as the sun sets and the evening approaches, the silhouette from that same tree casts scary shadows in the night. In Psalm 91:1, we discover the comfort and assurance that is associated with abiding in God's silhouette:

> [1] *He that dwelleth in the secret place of the most High shall abide under the shadow of the Almighty.*

The key word in this text is the word "dwelleth" which means to "abide or constantly remain." It suggests a continuous fellowship (with God). When you can identify the source of the shadow, there is no need to fear or to be *afraid*. Shade and shadows are dark areas but God's Shadow is our shade. When God shadows you, enjoy the shade of His Presence!

Dwelling in God is a decision. I lived in fear because I was not dwelling in God. The spirit of depression paralyzed me with a shadow of darkness. Even in this paralytic state, I knew what I was experiencing was not shade. Shade does not produce fear or confusion. In the darkness of depression, what used to be a shade of comfort became a shadow of confusion. In the darkness of depression, the familiar became unfamiliar and I saw strange shapes in the night.

While living in the shadows, it seemed as if the "brook dried up" right in front of me. The ministry was barely making it from week to week. After reviewing the weekly fiscal reports, the depression worsened. I felt God had left me in the wilderness (the land of just enough) and I wanted to be in Canaan (the land of more than enough)! Looking back, I should have been grateful that I was not in Egypt (the land of not enough). I will talk more about depression and economics later.

I was aimlessly wandering in a valley of calamity, chaos, and confusion. Depression was a dark cloud that came between God and me. Although dark, it wasn't nighttime. The Light of God's love was still shining but I had to escape the shadows. For years, I preached about God's increase but where was that increase now? Each week I examined, expounded, and expatiated on a Biblical Text that encouraged others to have faith while I had lost mine.

Suffering in silence eats away at you from within. How do I encourage others to have faith in a God I no longer had faith in? How do I keep selling a product I no longer believed in? It seemed as if God was uncaring, unconcerned, and uncommitted to my situation. I felt as if I was all alone in this spiritual quagmire and God was on some cosmic vacation a billion light years away on the other side of the universe. If God delivered others, why not me? Why was the manna that fell for others not falling for me? All I could ask was why, why, why? I did not realize it, but I was sliding deeper into the abyss of spiritual depression. Depression caused me to focus on what I was experiencing in the natural and not on what God was doing in the spiritual. Depression will have you seeing your life from the wrong perspective.

Depression under pressure brings you to a place of constant doubt, dismay, and defeat. From the pulpit, the pressure of failure was so constant that no matter how much I tried to preach, pray, or praise my way through, it seemed hopeless. The weight of the ministry was a constant companion that burdened me with feelings of inadequacy and defeat. My life was slipping away as I sank in the quicksand of depression.

Looks Can Be Deceiving

Looks can be deceiving. On a professional level, it appeared as if things could not have been better. I had completed seminary studies for my Master of Ministry degree and began studies in the Doctor of Ministry program. I was travelling across county, speaking, lecturing, and providing training at various religious and secular conferences and seminars. It is oxymoronic that at the same time I appeared to be succeeding outwardly, I was suffering inwardly. Allow me to speak into your life at this point about success. Don't fall into the trap of chasing success. Success is fleeting and to become obsessed with it is dangerous. In Kingdom work, God never tells us to be successful; He tells us to be faithful! In my season of depression, I discovered true success is the result of faithfulness. If you are faithful in serving God and seeking His Kingdom, success will find you!

I had not been totally faithful to God and was experiencing a slow and horrible death. My prayer life was nonexistent and for me, preaching was empty. I was a walking dead man and although I was existing, I was NOT living. I was NOT enjoying life. I was NOT enjoying my faith walk in Christ. I was NOT enjoying worship. I was NOT enjoying ministry. I was NOT enjoying what I was doing for God. I was NOT enjoying God.

I not only had to experience the valley of depression, I also had to escape it. Escaping this valley would be up to me and no one else. It was in the valley where I asked some hard questions, made some tough decisions, and was challenged like I had never been challenged before. For the first time, I felt dread. I was like a deer standing in the road blinded by the headlights of an oncoming vehicle: not a good scenario. All parties on the highway at that moment know there is going to be a collision. What is uncertain is how bad it's going to be.

Like that deer, I was blinded by my circumstances, dreadful, paralyzed by fear, and facing a slow death. My faith had vacated the premises and the spirit of fear had moved in. What I failed to realize is that doubt allowed the spirit of depression to paralyze me with a spirit of fear. Fear and Faith cannot co-exist in or occupy the same space. If I were to overcome this spirit of fear, I had to fight the spirit of depression. I could not continue in this valley, this low place, this crossroad.

I was shaken to the core of my being as everything I believed about God and His Word was challenged. I had no idea why my faith was under attack and simultaneously tempted, tested, and tried. It eventually got to the point where I had no desire to read the Bible. In seminary, I learned how to read the Bible for study, school, and sermon applications. I knew how to read, what to read, and where to read, but had no desire to read. I was empty, exhausted, and exacerbated in my faith-walk. I felt forsaken, abandoned, and completely alone. Forget that Jesus said "I will never leave or forsake you." Depression makes you delusional. The spirit of depression deceives you into believing everything is a lie except your truth. God had not abandoned me but that was not my truth. My truth was that I was going down for the count and as the waters of depression overwhelmed me, I was sinking to rise no more. I completely identified with the words of Jonah 2:2:

> *"...I cried by reason of mine affliction unto the LORD, and he heard me; out of the belly of hell cried I, and thou heardest my voice.*

Trust me when I say, God hears your cry and will help you overcome depression. The spirit of depression was toying with my emotions and getting the best of me. Although I felt abandoned, I knew I was saved and possessed the power of the Holy Spirit. My problem was remaining silent. I did not (and had not) opened my mouth to seek help or cry out to God. By remaining silent, my faith became dormant and needed activation. A dormant faith is a 'dead' faith until it is activated by the Word. According to Romans 10:17, faith comes alive by hearing God's Word. I needed to hear a Word that stirred up the gift God gave me. My faith needed to be activated so I could fight against the spirit of depression and forge ahead. It was not enough for me to preach, pray, and praise—I had to also press toward the mark! Like Paul, I had to press (persevere) toward the mark for the prize of the high calling of God in Jesus Christ (Philippians 3:14). God's mark and high calling for you is Jesus Christ. In your valley experience, keep pressing towards Christ! Through the power of Christ, you can and will overcome the spirit of depression. This is the ultimate lesson of valleys and crossroads – so don't stop fighting!

Valleys and Crossroads

The mountaintops of victory are seldom attained without travelling through the valleys of despair and suffering. Life is about valleys and crossroads. Depression was also my crossroad. I knew valleys were an inevitable part of life but I still did not like where I was. I had endured many struggles but this was different. As a child, I struggled with living in a troubled home and the divorce of my parents. As a husband, I struggled with the hurt and pains of my own failed marriage. As a son, I struggled with seeing my mother fight to overcome the perils of a major stroke. As a father, I struggled with overcoming the failures of parenting. As a Black man, I struggled with surviving in America. As a pastor, I struggled with the constant feelings of ineptitude, insufficiency, and inadequacy. How do you win a fight against yourself? What do you do when God is a silent observer standing in the distance?

Depression was oblivious to me being a pastor and did not care about my social class, financial status, or family pedigree. The spirit of depression and the spirit of fear does not care about you. These spirits are not concerned about your deliverance, they are committed to your destruction. In John 10:10, Jesus states that the thief comes to steal, kill, and destroy but He comes that you might have ABUNDANT LIFE. These two thieves stole my joy, killed my passion, and sought to destroy my life.

God is Love and wants you to live in favor and abundance. The valleys and crossroads of depression teach us that depression is a spirit of destruction. This spirit is colorblind to who we are and what we care about. This spirit cares nothing about our job, where we live, what we drive, our bank account, our ethnicity, or cultural background. It cares nothing about whether or not we go to church, believe in God, or profess Christ. Depression is the EEOC –an "Equal Employment Opportunity Companion" for all.

At some point, we will experience the headaches, heartaches, and hardships of the valley. The question is not *if we suffer*, but *when* and *how*. Whether the suffering is mental, emotional, physical, or spiritual – it is real and it is inevitable. Depression was not something I could see tangibly, but the pain was very real. Now that I had been attacked by the spirit of depression, was I going to react or respond? I needed to know the difference. To react meant taking immediate and involuntary action without thinking. To respond meant analyzing and assessing the situation to develop a strategic outcome. In the words of one anonymous writer: "Life is 10% of what happens to you and 90% of how you respond." The answer was obvious, I needed to find a way to respond to this attack without reacting!

Depression is mental and emotional suffering that is as real as any physical pain. Physical suffering is often diagnosed through a series of examinations and evaluations designed to identify the cause and find a cure. However, mental, emotional, and spiritual sufferings are much harder to diagnose and may last a lifetime. If I did not come out of this shadow, it could affect the rest of my life.

Depression shadowed me from God's Light and I needed it removed. The Light of God's love was still shining bright, but I had to come from the shadows.

Suffering is the price we pay for living in a world that is in constant decline. Nothing lasts forever and everything in this world (non-living, man-made, living, etc.) is decaying, declining, or dying. Non-living things decline, man-made things decay, and living things die. In my season of depression and suffering in silence, I had to dare to believe.

Daring to Believe

David's words in Psalm 27:13 are very personal and powerful for me. "I had fainted!" What powerful words! These three words suggest David had given up! This is the same man who walked through the "valley of the shadows of death", so you are in good company. If you feel like giving up, believe to see God's goodness. Never allow depression to stop you from believing!

I mentioned earlier that I was angry with God – very angry. However, God can handle your anger! I became angry when I stopped believing, hoping, and trusting in God. Although I was angry with God, my anger never stopped me from loving Him. Depression showed me God is not intimidated by anger. As a matter of fact, God used my anger to bring me to my breaking point. Your breaking point must precede your breakthrough. I don't know what your breaking point is, but you must get there before you can experience a breakthrough.

My breaking point occurred one Sunday morning while I was preaching. I was standing behind the Sacred Desk that morning and I remember thinking to myself (in the middle of my sermon), *"What the hell am I doing here."* While that might not seem so bad, that was not the problem. I knew there was a serious problem when I was within a fraction of a second from blurting out to the congregation what I was thinking to myself. Fortunately for me (and them) as the words were leaving my lips, God allowed me to catch myself. I was in trouble and knew I needed help.

Trouble, help, shame. I had experienced great shame and deep embarrassment about how I was feeling and what I was going through. Needless to say, my continued silence about my feelings did not help. Thankfully, I have come to understand depression and shame share a common thread: they survive and are strengthened through silence. Don't allow feelings of shame to silence your voice! Shame (like depression) loses power and control when you speak about it. The longer you remain silent about shame, the longer you are controlled by it.

Depression and shame were not my only problems. I was scared. The experience in the pulpit that Sunday scared me and caused me to go home and seek God. For the first time, I prayed and asked God for help. I finally did what I had avoided doing for so long. Like David, I had arrived at a point where I had fainted! I was at my breaking point and I could not take this anymore. Somehow, I had to dare to believe God. Daring to believe is not a time for nervous breakdowns; daring to believe is a time for noisy breakouts and new breakthroughs! If we dare to keep believing and trusting in God, nothing will be impossible.

A Divine Declaration: *Lord, I decree and declare through Your Name that in spite of my valleys and crossroads, You are the God of my salvation and that through your strength, I am made free!*

"Man that is born of a woman is of few days and full of trouble"
-Job 14:1

Chapter Three:

The Conflict of Suffering

***

A mother knows when something is wrong with her child (or children). I had not said anything to my mother about what I was experiencing. One day while talking with her about a totally different subject, (out of nowhere) she said, *"Larry, I know something is wrong and I know you are not going to tell me what it is. Take this from momma, a peace of mind is worth its weight in gold."* My soul was troubled and God used my mother's words to ring through my spirit like a floodgate from heaven. To this day I don't think my mother fully realizes or understands how God used her voice to speak to my faith. What she spoke into my life then is exactly what Jesus said to the raging Sea of Galilee so many years earlier, "Peace, be still."

Trouble is a part of life but I needed peace. Whether our days are many or few, one thing is certain – we will experience trouble. My trouble was the spirit of depression that had attacked my soul and spirit. I could not continue under the weight of such inner strain and conflict. If I really wanted peace, I could not depend on worldly peace. I needed a peace that transcended human understanding. I needed the perfect peace that only Christ could give because my life had become the fulfillment of the words of legendary gospel singer, James Cleveland:

Master, the tempest is raging!
The billows are tossing high!
The sky is o'ershadowed with blackness.
No shelter or help is nigh.
Carest thou not that we perish?
How canst thou lie asleep
When each moment so madly is threat'ning
A grave in the angry deep?

The winds and the waves shall obey thy will:
Peace, be still.
Whether the wrath of the storm-tossed sea
Or demons or men or whatever it be,
No waters can swallow the ship where lies
The Master of ocean and earth and skies.
They all shall sweetly obey thy will:
Peace, be still; peace, be still.
They all shall sweetly obey thy will:
Peace, peace, be still.

If I really wanted peace from the spiritual attack, I had to decide to trust God and leave the results to Him. I was in my eighth year of pastoral leadership and eight represents a new beginning at a new level. Eight years of pastoring had ushered me to a new level in ministry where I was experiencing a new beginning. I had come to a point where faith was all I had and trust was all I could do. I wrote earlier that depression comes when you try to resolve things that are beyond your control. Everything I was depressed about was beyond my control. The church was not my church and the people were not my people – whether people joined, stayed, or left; I needed to trust God for myself.

The lesson I learned at this "new level" of ministry was very clear: TRUST GOD!!! God uses valleys and crossroads as proving grounds. Why because proving precedes promotion. Depression was not my struggle with God – it was my struggle with how I perceived God in my situation. Depression taught me that in life, we are sometimes caught between the few and the full. It is there, in that lonely place where we must learn God for ourselves.

The Few and the Full

Job 14:1 sets the tone for how we are to view this paradigm called life – even during seasons of depression. In the eternal scheme of things, Job summarizes our existence in this world after birth as being "few days" and "full of trouble." Job understood that in the feebleness of our flesh, we are both few and full. In other words, we discover God in between the few and the full.

In discovering God, He uses life's struggles and sufferings to direct us to Himself. In Isaiah 6:1, Isaiah says it this way;

> *"In the year King Uzziah died (trouble), I saw (discovered) also the Lord; high lifted up and His train filled the temple (exalted)."*

In times of difficulty people will ask, "Where is God?" Isaiah addresses this question as he discovers God in his day of personal trouble. God is using your trouble as a way of introducing Himself to you. Trouble is God's way of saying "Hello, I'm God and I'm here to help you if you let me. Talk to me!" Trouble teaches you God was always there. Isaiah experiences serious trouble when his cousin (tradition) Uzziah dies. Like Job, Isaiah is caught between the few and the full. He is few in strength and filled with sorrow.

In his day of trouble, Isaiah uses the year of Uzziah's death as a reference point for when he discovers God. Before that, God is oblivious to Isaiah. God was always there but Isaiah didn't realize it. For Isaiah to see God as King, Uzziah had to die. Two kings cannot occupy the same throne and as King, God reigns when the people, places, and problems that come between you and He are removed. The shadow of depression has to be removed for you to see God. Although the Light is shining, depression keeps you from seeing God. Just as Uzziah's shadow prevented Isaiah from seeing God, depression's shadow prevented me from seeing God. Isaiah had to come out of the shadows to see God and so do we.

God uses life's low places to bring you higher in Him. It is in the valley where you discover the power of Christ. In Christ, you have complete joy and satisfaction. When Isaiah sees God in his day of trouble, he makes a profound and personal decision. Consider Isaiah 6:5-8:

> [5] *Then said I, Woe is me! for I am undone; because I am a man of unclean lips, and I dwell in the midst of a people of unclean lips: for mine eyes have seen the King, the LORD of hosts.*
>
> [6] *Then flew one of the seraphims unto me, having a live coal in his hand, which he had taken with the tongs from off the altar:*
>
> [7] *And he laid it upon my mouth, and said, Lo, this hath touched thy lips; and thine iniquity is taken away, and thy sin purged.*
>
> [8] *Also I heard the voice of the Lord, saying, Whom shall I send, and who will go for us? Then said I, Here am I; send me.*

After seeing God's awesome holiness and majestic power, Isaiah recognizes Him as King. In contrast, he sees himself as undone, unclean, and undeserving before God. Seeing God shows us the truth about ourselves. Uzziah's death was Isaiah's turning point and by exalting God, he has a breakthrough *in* his situation rather than a breakdown *about* his situation. What should have been Isaiah's breakdown became his breakthrough! What God does for Isaiah, He can do for you! In your season of depression, the most opportune time to discover God's presence is now.

Power without Purpose

Although I had counseled many people through seasons of despair, I had a very tough time dealing with my own. The weight of the ministry took a mental, physical, and spiritual toll on me. The added emotional trauma of depression made life a living hell. It is much easier helping others through their difficult times than it is dealing with your own. Over the years, I had preached so many sermons about faith, trust, and hope in God that I could almost quote the words verbatim. Now, those words were fleeting moments and lost memories of a distant past. To make matters worse, I continued suffering in silence.

Although I had reached my breaking point, my healing from depression started there, it did not end there. God does not always take things from you overnight – some things are progressive and occur over time. After reaching my breaking point, it was another five years before I was healed from depression. I'd cried out to God but was silent about what I was experiencing. I discovered that not only did I have to speak to God about my situation, I had to also speak to my situation about God. Since I had not spoken God's Word into my situation, I had work to do. Although my silent suffering was oblivious to others, it was deafening to me. How do I tell someone I was in a spiritual battle with depression? Even if told, how could they understand the spiritual toll depression had taken on my life?

I started preaching at age 15 and learned early that ministry is a lonely walk. I knew firsthand how cruel some people could be and the impact it can have on a pastor and his family. I also knew that some ecclesiastical colleagues were wolves in sheep clothing who (if they smelled blood), would do anything and everything in their power to use your moment of weakness against you.

Depression caused me to become a sad commentary for a preacher, a pastor, a person, and a professional. I'd lost my passion and preaching was no longer joyous. Consequently, I studied the Word of God without power and preached without purpose. I was like a parked car with its engine running and no place to go – *power without purpose.* It was only by God's grace that His Word accomplished its goal and did not come back empty. God is so faithful!! I am living proof that the emptiness of the witness does not equate to an empty Word. You may be empty today but that does not mean you have no value. God uses empty vessels! The power of God's Word has everything to do with God's might and not our own. I was empty but God's Word was filled with faith, favor, fellowship, and forgiveness. While preaching in my valley, God empowered His Word to be energetic, exciting, and edifying to the people. We can take no credit or glory for what God does – the power is of God, not us (II Corinthians 4:7). Because God is faithful, He sustained His Word in spite of my flaws. My flaws did not negate God's faithfulness.

As I encouraged others to stand firm in their faith, I faltered in mine. As time passed, my spirit became drained, deflated, and defeated. On Sundays, I preached two different sermons (8am and 11am) and sometimes three if we had to visit another church. In addition to performing my regular administrative duties as pastor, I was teaching weekly Bible study and in seminary conducting extensive reading, writing, and research projects towards my Doctorate. In spite of this, no one sensed I was depressed – or so I thought.

Pastor Walthour and Mr. Larry

I was suffering from a Dr. Jekyll and Mr. Hyde complex. Like Dr. Jekyll and Mr. Hyde, I was living with Pastor Walthour and Mr. Larry – two different persons struggling to exist in one body. While Pastor

Walthour was busy selling Jesus to others, Mr. Larry had lost faith in the product. How do you sell someone something you don't believe in? In public, I was Pastor Walthour – strong, secure, and stable! In private, I was Mr. Larry – wearied, wounded, and worn! My public display as Pastor Walthour was so good, I was convinced that no one knew I was depressed. I was so good at being Pastor Walthour that I could have received an Academy Award for my performance. It is amazing how we can deceive ourselves based on how we think about a circumstance or situation. As the Apostle Paul says in I Corinthians 10:12,

"if any man thinks he is standing firm, let him take heed lest he fall."

I stood firm on what I convinced myself to believe. I was good at fooling others, but not at fooling myself. I should have listened to the latter part of Paul's advice: *"...let him take heed lest he fall."* Depression had deceived me into believing I was standing when I had already fallen. I was well aware of who Pastor Walthour was, but who was this Mr. Larry?

There are two little people in our life named Janelle and Kali. They are my grandchildren. When they were much younger and would see me, they had an uncanny and endearing way of calling me "Mr. Larry" in almost perfect unison. It was the cutest thing when you heard it (I really believe they practiced this for perfection). If I were at a distance and they saw me, they would both come running with arms flinging and clothes flying saying, "Mr. Larry, Mr. Larry!!! Hey Mr. Larry!!" Of course I would smile and yell back at them, "Hey!! Little People!!!" I used to pick them up but that is becoming more difficult with age. It was not what they said that's the caveat, it's how they said it. They said "Mr. Larry" in a way that embraces family, friendship, and familiarity. It says that they know me.

Like Janelle and Kali, I discovered that some people <u>knew</u> me. There were members who sensed something was wrong but didn't know how to address it or ask me about it. I am certain that if asked, I would have denied that anything was wrong. It's not easy allowing others to see you vulnerable. This becomes even more difficult when you are unsure about your confidants, constituents, comrades. Are they assigned to you and can they handle your vulnerability? When you are vulnerable, your feelings and emotions can trick you into believing that God is far away and indifferent to your silence, sufferings, and supplications. I have learned that in times like these, God is much closer than you think.

Bad Things; Good People

In my season of depression, I would often ask myself, "Why has this happened to me?", "What did I do to deserve this?", "Why me?" I was stuck on the question, "Why do bad things seem to happen to good people?" By my standards, I believed I was a pretty good person and a good pastor. I also felt I had legitimate grounds upon which to question God. Before I proceed on, let me pause to say that questioning God is not a sin. There is no place in recorded Scripture that says questioning God is a Sin. Abraham questioned God, Moses questioned God, David questioned God, Elijah questioned God, and on the cross, even Jesus questioned God. I questioned God out of anger and a lack of understanding. I would even dare say that I moved from questioning God to interrogating Him. I wanted answers because I felt I did not deserve this. Why would a God who says He loves me, allow me to end up here in this dismal, dry, and destitute place? Depression had me in a shadow of darkness and a cave of despair. I didn't understand the move of God because I saw things from the wrong perspective and asked the wrong questions. Looking back, a more appropriate question would have been: "Why the *innocent*?"

It was not so much that I was a good person, I was innocent. Since humanity is flawed by Sin, God is the Ultimate Good in this world (Mark 10:18). As individuals, the good we do is from a sinful position and therefore flawed. Listen to what Jesus says about this situation in Mark 10:17–18:

> ***17****And when he was gone forth into the way, there came one running, and kneeled to him, and asked him, Good Master, what shall I do that I may inherit eternal life?*
>
> ***18****And Jesus said unto him, Why callest thou me good? There is none good but one, that is, God.*

In Romans 3:10–12, the Apostle Paul echoes the words of Christ when he states the following:

> ***10****As it is written, There is none righteous, no, not one:*
>
> ***11****There is none that understandeth, there is none that seeketh after God.*
>
> ***12****They are all gone out of the way, they are together become unprofitable; there is none that doeth good, no, not one.*

When talking to the rich young ruler, Jesus declares God to be the Ultimate Standard of what is good in this world. The Apostle Paul confirms this when he declares there is none who is righteous and seeks God's will. Since we are not morally good by God's standard, we are therefore innocent. By innocent, I am not saying we are sinless, perfect, guiltless, and without fault—I am simply saying that we sometimes end up in valleys, caves, and shadowy places by no fault of our own. These experiences are often beyond our control and have nothing to do with us.

Bad things (what we consider to be bad) happen to *all* people. Good and bad are terms we use in relation to our feelings, emotions, and experiences. We call what we like "good" and what we don't like "bad." Our view has little (if anything) to do with God's view. As we mature, we understand the times we didn't realize that some things we thought were good for us was actually bad and some things that we thought were bad were actually good.

From my perspective, depression was a bad thing because I didn't like it, understand it, or want it. From God's perspective, depression was a tool for my good. In my ignorance, I erroneously called what God was using for my greater good a bad thing. Depression was not good to me, but it was for my good. I had to believe and trust God with my greater good. Let God handle your good! I didn't see it then, but God was using what I saw as a bad situation (depression) for my good.

Since God has healed me from depression, I can now speak life to those fighting the spirit of depression. If it were not for depression, I would not have had a life experience that challenged me to keep hoping and trusting in God. Sometimes it is difficult to see God working through pain and sufferings. In my silence and sufferings, I learned that God was still Sovereign. God brought deliverance through that which was meant to destroy and defeat me. Only God can use depression as a tool for deliverance. I can testify that although depression was not to my good, God used it for my good! I decree and declare over your life today that depression will not be your demise! I declare your assurance in knowing that like the Apostle Paul in Romans 8:28:

> [28]*And we know that all things (the good, the bad, and the ugly) work together for the greater good of those who love the Lord and who are the called according to His purpose.*

Trusting God's perspective of your situation requires a mental shift. How you think is detrimental to your survival. You become what you think you are. As a man (or woman) thinks in their heart, so is he. A mental shift is necessary because our actions, feelings, attitudes, etc. are connected to how we think. As you move forward, I pray that God renews your mind so you can walk by faith and not by sight. Don't allow yourself to become a prisoner of your thoughts – let God renew your mind!

Renewing the Mind

The spirit of depression uses your mind against you. When depressed, it is important that you control your thinking. I had to adjust how I perceived and thought about what I was experiencing. Your mind is the enemy's battleground to attack you with destructive thoughts, emotions, imaginations, and strongholds. Because the mind is such a powerful tool, it has to be renewed before we are changed. If the mind (our thinking) changes, we change. Consider what the Apostle Paul says in Romans 12:2:

> [2] *And be not conformed to this world: but be ye transformed by the renewing of your mind, that ye may prove what is that good, and acceptable, and perfect, will of God.*

Taking authority over your mind is not the same as renewing it. We take authority but it is the Spirit that renews. To renew means to make new again. The mind must be renewed because the spirit of depression conforms you to worldly thinking. I believe mind renewal is connected to how much you give yourself to God. The more you give yourself to God, the more He renews your thought process. God wants to free you from the perils of worldly thinking! Christian Life Coach Derik Wilder offers some practical steps you can take to start the process of controlling your mind. I will paraphrase his steps at this point.

Step #1 Limit Unhealthy Thoughts by Writing them Down. When destructive feelings or emotions such as anger, jealously, feelings of inadequacy, envy, sadness, despair, etc. arise, a subtle thought is at work. In 2 Corinthians 10:5, the Apostle Paul instructs us to capture our thoughts by submitting them to the Word of God. When your thoughts rebel against God's Word, you become an easy target for depression. You must destroy every thought that rejects God's Truth and place every impulse, emotion, and wandering thought into a mind framed and shaped by Christ. Any thought that rejects/rebels against God's Truth must be taken captive.

Step #2 Limit Lies (thoughts) by Writing them Down. Identify the lie or thought that caused you emotional harm, write it down, and ask yourself what caused it. Where did this destructive thought or lie come from and what caused it? Thoughts like these race through your mind extremely fast so becoming aware and attentive when they occur is a must. These are worldly thoughts that create destructive emotions that are planted in your mind by the spirit of depression.

Step #3 Liberate Truth: Write Down Replacing Thoughts (truth). Once you identify the lie and its destructive emotions, replace it with Truth. Replacing lies with Truth is a part of sanctification (the process of transformation). In St. John 17:17, Jesus teaches this when He prays, *"Sanctify them by the Truth, Thy Word is Truth."* Replacing lies with Truth means injecting God/Christ (Who is Truth) into your thought process by simply writing down the opposite thought of the lie.

Step #4 Lastly, Constantly Read Replacement Thoughts (truth). It is important to know that these four steps DO NOT renew the mind. Though it makes a great difference, replacing lies with truth is *revelation*, not *renewal.* Revelation is "the process of God making Himself known to people (Holman's Bible Dictionary)." Renewing the mind is the Spirit of God working in you to develop the mind of Christ. Replacing lies with truth is injecting the knowledge of God (Truth) to confront the mental lies attacking you. Truth comes from God and when truth is revealed, the opportunity for renewal begins. When your mind is renewed, better days will come.

Better Days are Coming

Sometimes it seems like innocence suffers while evil gets a free pass. It was once said that, *"the truth has to hitch-hike while a lie takes a luxury jet."* Time and time again it seems as if people of good-will leave this world quickly while the evil and wicked live forever. Even if evil seems to get by, God will judge it in the end. Depression was an evil force that God's Spirit empowered me to overcome. I have learned that Truth will be justified – even if it has to go through Calvary. In Psalm 73:2-4, David expresses this paradox when he proclaimed:

> [2] *My foot had nigh slipped when I saw the prosperity of the wicked.*
> [3] *For I was envious at the foolish, when I saw the prosperity of the wicked.*
> [4] *For there are no bands in their death: but their strength is firm.*

It is hard to see the wicked prosper while you are in constant pain and suffering. For those who believe and trust in God, this can become a very slippery slope. Life can be a very difficult and unforgiving journey and handling slippery slopes are never easy. For me, depression was my slippery slope and it is a slope I still fight to avoid today. Like David, I watched in pain as others (the wicked and other believers alike) continued prospering as I was in peril. My peril had grown to a place where I began to magnify my grief and minimize God. If you are not careful, depression will have you believing that God is the antithesis to what the Bible says He is! Despite how severe the situation, you must believe better days are coming. My hope was fueled by a faith that still believed. Even though I had stopped believing with my mind; in my heart, my faith still believed! In spite of how dire the situation, trust God enough to believe.

As I stated before, I had a serious problem with God. I was what

I would call a MESS! The spirit of depression had me bound **M**entally, **E**motionally, **S**piritually, and **S**ocially. Like David, when I saw others prospering around me (saved and unsaved alike), I sank further into depression. Depression blinded me to fully appreciating God's abundant grace and active goodness in my own experience. My inner conflict with depression numbed me to God's presence in my life. Depression is the inner conflict of the soul and my soul was where I experienced my greatest and most intense conflict – the conflict with my inner self. Like Job, I was filled with joy and sorrow.

A Divine Declaration: *Lord, I decree and declare through Your Name that in spite of my conflicts of sufferings, I will continue to trust in Your loving kindness and abundant grace.*

Note: Derek Wilders' complete commentary can be found at Lives Transforming https://www.livestransforming.com/renewing-the-mind/

For the love of money is the root of all evil: which while some coveted after, they have erred from the faith, and pierced themselves through with many sorrows."
-I Timothy 6:10

Chapter Four:

A Misguided Faith: Socio-Economics

***

My brink with spiritual collapse was not a phenomenon – I was not the first nor will I be the last to experience depression. We will all experience some form of depression at one time or another. Depression may be a part of life but you cannot allow yourself to collapse under its weight. Collapses can be disastrous. In 1929, the world experienced the greatest economic collapse in history. As stock markets collapsed and people lost their jobs, life savings, retirements, properties, and other investments, the world entered what became known as the Great Depression. For approximately 10 years (1929-1939), the United States and the rest of the world existed in a state of economic crisis.

The global collapse of the U.S. and world economies also lead to personal collapses in the lives of ordinary people. As more and more people lost their equity and worldly wealth, suicides, homicides, and other social tragedies increased worldwide. For many, their misguided faith in the world's economic systems caused great sorrow. In Ecclesiastes 1:9, King Solomon declares the following:

> *The thing that hath been, it is that which shall be; and that which is done is that which shall be done: and **there is no new thing under the sun***

These words are a reminder that what we face today, others have faced before. History is an epic narrative of life's repeating lessons. Solomon's claim that there is no new thing under the sun is his way of saying, "It's coming up again." Like during the Great Depression, people are still losing what they have worked for their entire lives and collapsing under the weight of trying to make ends meet. The average person is only one or two paychecks from being homeless and most of us are just one hospital visit from Headache Avenue and Hardship Lane. One unfortunate situation can change the course of your life forever. Like Job, some people have lost everything overnight — those who appeared to have it all one moment were broke, busted, and bankrupt the next.

As a pastor, this takes on an even greater burden because most members don't realize how much we feel their pain. When church members hurt, I hurt because what happens in their lives directly and indirectly impacts my life and the ministry. In my season of depression I learned that life is a spiritual roller coaster upon which we cannot afford to ride on the fringes of the emotional.

It's the Economy—Stupid!

I mentioned earlier that I would discuss ministry and the economy later. Depression helped me understand there is a Kingdom connection between the minister, the ministry, and money. This connection is interchangeable and cannot be separated. Although God is the Ultimate Giver and Provider, what happens in the local, state, national, and global economies impact congregational giving and the church's ability to do Kingdom work. These various economies directly affect how I minister to the church, the congregation, and the community. Functional ministry is a sustained economic investment. Without members making a personal commitment to sustained economics, church ministry becomes impossible. I did not realize how much the church's economy would impact my bout with depression.

Money and ministry are inseparable. It takes money to manage and maintain church ministry and to facilitate efficient and effective church growth. Many people have tried to make pastors and churches feel guilty about asking for money. Any pastor will tell you it takes money to provide staffing, training, operations, ministries, and other functions. The church, like any other business or organization must have funds to provide spiritual service in a material world. If the church is to carry out its Kingdom mandate, it requires giving, receiving, and investing.

Let me say unequivocally that there is nothing wrong with money, having money, making money, asking for money, or receiving money. Money is a means to an end and a symbolic way of exchange that answers all things (Ecclesiastes 10:19). However, in ministry we must be very careful when dealing with money because it becomes dangerous to fall in love with it. As the Apostle Paul suggests in I Timothy 6:10, it is the love of money (not money) that is the root of all evil. The love of money is destructive and has caused much sorrow (depression) for those who have abandoned their faith in God. The love of money is closely connected to depression and sorrow.

As a pastor, I see the relation between spiritual pressures and social problems. The spirit of depression can use the lack of sufficient finance to bait you into a depressive state. Giving (or the lack thereof) is directly connected to the various conditions and experiences of those to whom I preach each week. It is very difficult preaching divine prosperity to a congregation who is struggling with daily provision. In the church, true prosperity must become a collective journey wherein the pastor is not the only one who prospers in the ministry. Prosperity is a state of existence and if you are not careful, the spirit of depression will use your surroundings to lure you into the state of depression. If you live in a place of depression, it's easy to fall into the trap of depression.

We must offer a message of hope to those living in depression. This does not mean we offer a "pie in the sky" religion based on emotions. Having "pie in the sky" is worthless when your plate on earth is empty. Our message of hope must include ministry and money. Without money, people cannot live, survive, or take care of their families. Without money, communities become dangerous and riddled with crime. Without money, churches are hindered from meeting ministry needs, supporting missions, and doing Kingdom work.

For a pastor, lack of giving from the congregation can be devastating. It sends a multitude of messages – none of which are good. From a financial perspective, I felt helpless and hopeless in meeting the needs of those I was called to serve. As a mid-sized church, we were at a place of fiscal and economic stagnation. This was not a good place to be. Church finances weighed heavily on me because as I reviewed the weekly, quarterly, and annual income reports for the ministry, I knew we should be doing better for a church with a membership our size. Had the membership stopped giving or were they no longer able to give?

South Florida is not the easiest place to pastor a church. It is a playground, not praying ground. The cost of living is high, wages are minimal, and there are too many things competing with God's Kingdom. In addition to the malls, the beaches, the night life, the festivals, the arts, the professional sports, the tourist attractions, and the weather, you must also compete with members not attending worship and the challenge of church growth. South Florida is considered paradise and it's not easy getting people prepared for heaven when they are already living in paradise. Giving and growth goes hand in hand and for whatever reason, the church was at a place of fiscal stagnation as the people *seemed* to have plateaued in their fiscal giving and support.

I used the word seemed because everything is not what it seems to be. The people had not stopped giving because they had lost confidence in me or the vision (as I had supposed), but because of other challenges in the economy at the time. Those challenges caused a trickledown effect that impacted church giving. God loves persons who are joyous about giving; teaching about giving is one thing but trusting God to give is another. Trusting God with finances in hard times is not so easy when you are debt-laden and facing major fiscal challenges. It is during these times that it seems as if the church has the most needs and the members have less to give. Although people may *love* God, the reality is that they *live* by paying their mortgage/rent, water, car note, gas, lights, food, phone, electricity, clothes, insurance, cable, and other household expenses. As I said, South Florida is not the easiest place for ministry growth. If people are not committed to budgeting their own finances, tithing/giving to a church is just another bill with little or no priority. As I struggled to cast the vision and encourage membership participation, the spirit of depression continued to overwhelm me. As a pastor, I was learning a lesson that was rooted in the words of James Carville, former campaign strategist for President Bill Clinton: it's the economy—stupid!

The Greed Principle

Greed is one of the primary reasons people struggle with giving. The greed principle is very subtle and powerful. Greed is one of the

Seven Deadly Sins and is rooted in the love of money. Because of greed, this world is not what God created it to be. God created this world with more than enough resources for everyone to enjoy a prosperous, productive, and purposeful life. Because of greed, this will never happen for everyone. In the words of Christ, "the poor you will have with you always (Matthew 26:11)." Greed prohibits equity because it never satisfies. Enough is never enough and the more you have, the more you want. Greed corrupts every aspect of our lives—political, educational, social, spiritual, and fiscal.

Part of my struggle was trying to overcome the spirit of greed that was trying to influence the hearts of the people I was asking to give. My new shoes or the building fund? That new dress, or Sunday's offering? That upcoming concert or the church anniversary? There will always be something competing with you for what belongs to God.

Each week, I am presented with the task of finding a way to holistically minister to those who are living in a frustrated, fragmented, fractured, and fiscally oppressed society. Due to the hardships with the economy, many of our supportive members started relocating their families to other states to find work or enjoy retirement. In either case, when families relocate and people lose their jobs and/or are demoted, it has a direct impact on the life of the ministry and the economy of the church. Because the economy has a direct impact on the membership and the ministry, it also has a direct impact on me – the minister.

Understanding where you are

Part of overcoming depression is understanding where you are. In this country, we are bombard with the luxuries of tangible affluence. This within itself can become depressing and/or lead to depression. In America, the more tangible affluence you have, the more successful you are. Just look at the various television programs and the music that is marketed to our youth and society. Everything is centered on money, success, fame, and fortune. Although there is nothing wrong with any of these things, we must keep them in perspective and put them in the proper context. The constant pursuit for material wealth and instant gratification is a leading cause for depression. As I stated earlier, when I focused on others, the depression worsened and created a domino effect that made me feel more hopeless.

When money becomes your motive and your motivation, your world becomes imbalanced. As I observe the socio-economic landscape of today's society, I see people losing faith in God and giving in to feelings of despair and hopelessness. As people lose their hope, Satan has masterfully strangled the respect and relevancy of the church. The greed and corruption of our society has created an environment where people feel as if things are worse – not better. I see this reality each week in the lives of those who attend church on Sundays. Churches across the country are seeing declining faces in the pews. People attend church less and less and for those who do attend, Sunday worship has become a pep rally experience. For many believers, Sunday's have become a feel good service and a means by which they can just make it through the week.

Understanding where we are means realizing our social fabric is so poisoned with greed and instant gratification that it permeates every aspect of society – including church. I experienced this phenomena personally and professionally. I soon learned that many of those I was preaching to on Sundays were so influenced by greed and instant gratification during the week that it became hard to give. It is this same greed and instant gratification that has contributed greatly to the pain and suffering seen today.

In retrospect, I realize the socio-economic conditions of South Florida had created a misguided faith within the congregation. This was not only true with the church, it is also true within the context of the larger community. It was problem that could only be solved through strategic growth and sustained giving. Sadly, this constant pursuit of greed and instant gratification has caused many to have self-inflected wounds. This is what Paul means when he says that those who went after money has pierced themselves with many sorrows. The most painful wounds I experienced during depression were the self-inflicted ones. As I continued suffering in silence, I came to a place of hopelessness. My story is not much different from yours or many others – including many who serve in the pulpit. Even as you read these words, there are many pastors who are depressed in their pulpits. Sadly, many who suffer are like me – they suffer *in silence.*

As I continued preaching a Rhema word to the membership that was relative to the times, it became increasingly clear that many in the congregation were barely making it. How could I financially grow the church with a membership that had flat-lined in their giving? Again, South Florida is an area of the country where the wage income does not match the cost of living. I had become so sensitive to the struggles of the members that their pain had become mine. As contributions flat-lined, I soon understood that giving had become a financial strain on the congregation.

I would often join other pastors to "meet for coffee" and share various experiences that we faced in our ministries. In talking with them and sharing our stories, I discovered that I was not alone in what I was facing. As we talked about our ministry experiences, I found out that although things were tough, I was a lot better off than I had realized.

No Pain, No Gain

Never make a permanent decision on a temporary situation. Although depression was personally painful, it did not become permanent. Pain is a part of God's process and for me, depression was personal pain. There is a special kind of joy in knowing that God uses your pain to produce great gain in your life. Sometimes you must endure the pain so that you can enjoy the gain – as we like to say in religious circles: no cross, no crown! In spite of the bad economy, mediocre giving, struggles with the ministry, and other obstacles I faced in my personal and professional life, there was a comfort in knowing things were not as bad as I had thought. I had allowed my misery to define my outlook on ministry. While some ministries were relocating, reducing services, cutting back on staff, or shutting down completely, God had still allowed us to manage our resources, maintain what we had, and stay afloat.

It is impossible to know why a person walks the way they walk until you spend some time walking in their shoes. Looking at a situation and judging it from the outside is far easier than having to experience that situation from within. I allowed myself to judge God through the darkness of the shadow and not the light of His love. Depression was still between me and God and I was still fighting to come to His Light. Although I needed to come out of the shadow of depression, I was still learning valuable lessons while there. God can teach you no matter where you are! My bout with depression taught me how to empathize and sympathize with others. Through a spirit of empathy, I am able to relate to what others are feeling when they are experiencing hard times. Through a spirit of sympathy, I am able to give them God's comfort in knowing that things will get better. No matter how bad things might be in the severity of the moment, I have discovered that God is still all good, at all times, and in all situations!

A Divine Declaration: *Lord, I decree and declare that through Your Name, Your Holy Spirit will transform my misguided faith into a faith that makes You the focus of my desire.*

"Being confident of this very thing, that he which hath begun a good work in you will perform it until the day of Jesus Christ:"
– Philippians 1:6

Chapter Five:

Enduring the Process

***

Let me be clear. St. Andrew Baptist Church or its membership was NOT the cause of my depression. This is a good congregation with faithful, loving people. Like any church, we had challenges. However, I was not depressed *because of* the church, I just happen to be depressed *while at* the church. In addition to many other factors that weighed on me, my life was out of balance at the time. If I were to come out of this season of depression, I would have to undergo and endure the process. Everything has a process. As a matter of fact, God does everything by plan, process, and procedure. Endurance challenges you to go through the process. Sometimes it is difficult to endure the heat – especially when you are in the fire! In the heat of depression, I was under fire and in the fire at the same time. God's process is connected to His timing. A process is defined as a sequential series of steps and/or actions that are taken to achieve a particular result. Based on this definition, a process is strategic. I have learned that God is strategic and pays great attention to detail. As you journey into the Light of God's love, just know that everything connected to a process is in some way a part of that process.

Enduring my season of depression was very difficult. It seemed as if the more I wanted to get out, the longer I stayed in. Whether or not this was of my own doings or of God's, I am not sure. What I am sure of is that God was in the process. Even when the process is prolonged, God is still present. This is a sure indication of God's faithfulness to us in tough and tempestuous times. According to Psalm 16:11, in God's presence is fullness of joy and at His right hand are pleasures forevermore.

For me, another part of the process was finding a way to pastor while depressed. Depression was taking a heavy toll on me mentally, physically, emotionally, and spiritually. Everything in my life was a struggle. I struggled with my ministry, I struggled with my calling, I struggled with my assignment, I struggled with my relationships, I struggled with my expectations, I struggled with my self-assurance, I struggled with my life, I struggled with living, and I struggled with God. I even struggled with getting up in the morning. Sometimes I would wake up in the mornings and just lay in bed staring at the ceiling. There was no passion or motivation for anything in my life. Everything was empty, void, and seemingly without purpose.

Pastoring in Pain

I was a pastor in pain. It has been eloquently said time and time again that "Hurt people, hurt people." When you are in pain, it becomes easy to inflict pain to others. I have found that pain is an important part of our humanity and a necessary part of life. Pain is defined as physical, mental, emotional, or spiritual suffering and/or discomfort caused by illness or injury. Pain can be devastating and have lasting consequences.

There are two ways to deal with pain – internally or externally. Most people who internalize their pain have no idea of the devastating consequences and impact it can have. Suffering in silence is a common disorder that is extremely dangerous and very destructive. By nature, I am an introverted person. It is quite natural for me to internalize my pain - whether it be emotional, mental, physical, or spiritual. While this might be a better approach at times, in most cases it causes isolation, frustration, loneliness, stress, and many other problems.

If internalizing pain is so destructive, why do we do it? The main reason is to avoid becoming a bother and a burden to others. I (like many others) was taught to believe internalization was equivalent to strength. In doing so, I convinced myself that internalizing my pain was a much better way of handling it. I soon realized that pain has no respect of persons. In my service as a pastor, I needed to embrace my own pain so I could be empathetic towards others. Depression is an isolated kind of pain that leads to violation. Depression violates you by isolating you from what is and is not real. Depression made me feel as if no one cared – *not real.* It made me feel as if I was alone – *not real.* It made me feel like I was a failure – *not real.* It made me feel hopeless – *not real.* It made me feel abandoned – *not real.* Regardless of what was not real during my season of depression, the one thing that became apparently real to me was that I was pastoring in pain.

Perceiving the Problem

I was oblivious to depression until I came to a breaking point. I did not realize I was depressed until I realized I was depressed. Since I had not realized I was depressed, I had no way of perceiving the problem. How you choose to address (or not address) a problem indicates how mature or immature you are at handling it. When you address problems immaturely, there is a great possibility you will worsen the situation. Depression taught me that not addressing my pain, is a way of addressing it. I learned the hard way that ignoring pain is to handle it in a destructive way. Not choosing *is* a choice. If you chose not to use your voice to address depression, you are choosing to suffer in silence.

I can speak from experience that suffering in silence is not the answer. Internalizing pain causes more harm than good. Silence amplified my suffering. I had to learn how to handle my pain externally by giving voice to my pain in a calm, cool, and collective manner. I would have to now find a way to calmly voice my concerns at the appropriate times. This was uncomfortable for me in the beginning and it still is today. You would think that since I am a speaker, this would be easy. This could not be further from the truth. Sometimes the simplest tasks are the most difficult. Simple words are not so simple to say. Although I still struggle in this area of awkward discomfort, the more I give voice to my pain the more natural it becomes.

Processing the Pain

Pain is not always a bad thing. Sometimes pain is an indicator that things are functioning properly. If you or I happened to burn ourselves and felt no pain, that would be a serious problem! While I would not say that pain is a good thing, I would say that not all pain is bad. When it comes to processing pain, nothing *seems* more rewarding than overcoming something in your own strength. If you are trying to overcome depression in your own strength, you are already in a position of defeat. The spirit of depression will not allow you to overcome it with your own strength. You must have a strength more powerful than your own. We often are deceived into thinking that we are toughest when we make it on our own. In Philippians 4:13, the Apostle Paul declares

"I can do all things through Christ who strengthens me."

You must draw from the strength God gives you through Christ and others. Sometimes God sends your strength in Christ through other people. I believe God uses social workers, mental health counselors, therapists, pastors, intercessors, clinicians, and many other professionals to help bring a depressed person into healing and wholeness. This does not mean depending on others for every little thing. Never feel guilty about drawing strength from others during times of dismay, discouragement, distress, and depression. Sometimes that strength is a listening ear, a helping hand, a kind word, or a simple prayer. However, overcoming depression means drawing on your personal strength while using God's direct strength to guide you through the situation.

The Power of Prayer and Praise

There is power in prayer and praise. In my journey to overcome depression, these were two of my most powerful tools. I eventually talked with God to get a better perspective of myself. I had to rediscover prayer as a vital part of my faith walk. Depression is an attack on your internal being but prayer connects you with the Eternal. Prayer allows you to get in tune with God so you can have a better view of yourself. It involves more than just looking within. It involves looking up to a God who is omnipotent, omniscient, and omnipresent. I believe God uses prayer differently than what we think. We think God hears our prayers and makes all the changes. This type of thinking eliminates our part in the process of miraculous change. Faith without works is dead. Faith and works go hand in hand.

There were times I didn't want to pray, praise, or read my Bible. Depression had me at a place where I didn't know what to say to God or how to pray. I was angry with God and bitter. Although I knew I could pray and still believed in the power of prayer, I did not want to pray. Talking *to* God is not the same as talking *with* God. When I did decide to talk with God, I began to see prayer from a totally different perspective. Through prayer, I learned how God changes me and uses me to change things. Although change starts from within, we must do the work. When we pray, God changes us inwardly so we can be used by Him to change things outwardly. This is how God works in this world.

On the other side of prayer is praise. Prayer is talking with God while praise is thanking God. Our son Olvins has a very calm persona. No matter what seems to be happening with him or around him, he has a sense of sheer calm. Even when his life is chaotic, he demonstrates calm. He has the type of persona that calms others in tense and troubling situations. I would say this is a unique God given ability. In fact, that's exactly what happens on the other side of prayer. When you pray to God in the midst of your trouble, He gives you a calm and collective spirit of praise. Your praise is the collective calm that is on the other side of the chaos!

I am thankful to God that in my season of depression, I never lost my praise. I lost the will to pray but I still had a praise. I lost the will to work, but I still had a praise. I lost the will to walk, but I still had a praise. I even lost the will to witness, but I still had a praise. In my season of pain, God kept me with a praise! Tremaine Hawkins says it this way:

I've lost some good friends along life's way
Some loved ones departed in heaven to stay
But thank God I didn't lose everything
I've lost faith in people who said they cared
In time of my crisis they were never there
But in my disappointment, in my season of pain
One thing never wavered, one thing never changed

I never lost my hope
I never lost my joy
I never lost my faith
But most of all, I never lost my praise

I've let some blessings slip away
When I lost my focus and went astray
But thank God I didn't lose everything
I lost possessions that were so dear
I lost some battles walking in fear
But in the midst of my struggles, in my season of pain
One thing never wavered, one thing never changed

I never lost my hope
I never lost my joy
I never lost my faith
But most of all, I never lost my praise

There will be times in life when praise is all you've got! In my season of depression, all I had was a praise! Like Tremaine, I can testify that I never lost my praise! Praise His Holy Name!!! In my depression, my disappointment, my dismay, and even in my discouragement, I found a way to praise God. Don't stop praising God because there is power in praise! The Word of God illustrates praise as a weapon. In II Chronicles 20:22, it states the following:

> *"As they began to sing and praise, the Lord set ambushes against the men of Ammon and Moab and Mount Seir who were invading Judah, and they were defeated."*

When you sing and praise God through your pain, God will ambush your enemies and turn things around!! The spirit of depression was an enemy that had invaded my life but through praise, God set an ambush against depression and turned my life around! If He did it for me, He can do it for you right now! The last time I checked, my God still inhabits the praises of His people and a praise that comes from a place of pain is a powerful praise!

Please don't misunderstand what I am saying because I am not suggesting that praise is a substitute for prayer. Nothing is a substitute for prayer – besides God's Word, prayer is our most powerful weapon. Prayer can go where we can't go, do what we can't do, and change what we can't change. If you or I lose the will, desire, or fortitude to pray, the Holy Spirit (and others) can pray on our behalf (Romans 8:26). In seasons of distress, the Holy Spirit (and others) can pray for you but they cannot praise God for you. The Holy Spirit (and others) can praise God with you (Luke 10:21-24; Psalm 34:3), but they cannot praise God for you. When it comes to praising God, nobody can praise God for you but you! You must praise God for yourself! Praise Him and Bless His Name!! If you are in a season of depression, you must find a way to praise God for yourself. For me, depression personalized my praise and gave it purpose. Through it, I developed a personal praise that kept me going even when I felt like giving up.

Proclamation through the Pain

Our words have immense and unimaginable power. Life and death is in the power of the tongue (Proverbs 18:21). This passage makes it very clear that our words can bring life or death into a situation. Our words are so powerful they can appease wrath or generate anger (Proverbs 15:1). It is amazing how something so small can have so much power and be at the center of so much attention. Consider this passage of Scripture from James 3:5-10:

> [5] *Even so the tongue is a little member, and boasteth great things. Behold, how great a matter a little fire kindleth!*

[6] And the tongue is a fire, a world of iniquity: so is the tongue among our members, that it defileth the whole body, and setteth on fire the course of nature; and it is set on fire of hell.

[7] For every kind of beasts, and of birds, and of serpents, and of things in the sea, is tamed, and hath been tamed of mankind:

[8] But the tongue can no man tame; it is an unruly evil, full of deadly poison.

[9] Therewith bless we God, even the Father; and therewith curse we men, which are made after the similitude of God.

[10] Out of the same mouth proceedeth blessing and cursing. My brethren, these things ought not so to be.

As I journeyed through my season of depression, I failed to realize how faithful God had been to me through the power of His Word. As a pastor for the past 23 years, each week I have the privilege of preaching God's Word to a waiting congregation. Although depression had me at a low place, I knew the power of God's Word. If God's Word worked for me during depression, it will also work for you. Trust me when I tell you, God's Word is able to deliver you from the spirit of depression. In depression, I experienced the words of Isaiah 55:11.

[11] So shall my word be that goeth forth out of my mouth: it shall not return unto me void, but it shall accomplish that which I please, and it shall prosper in the thing whereto I sent it.

I know from experience that God's Word will accomplish whatever He sends it to do. Whatever God declares by His Word, He performs through His Word. There is no promise, plan, or purpose from God that goes unfulfilled. God's Word is like a boomerang; it goes out and returns with ferocity and power. When we speak God's Word over our depression, there is no way it can return to Him void (empty, worthless, without purpose). God's Word will always accomplish His desired intent.

God's Word Completes His Work

Philippians 1:6 testifies that God completes His work in us. In other words, God finishes what He's started. In my life, He uses (not used) depression to continue perfecting His unfinished work in me. This unfinished work is reserved unto the day (or time) of Jesus Christ. During my season of depression, God was working in me, on me, and through me at the same time. What I did not realize at the time was that by preaching God's Word and speaking life to others, I was also speaking life over my own depression. I did not realize that God was using the sermons I was preaching to others, to speak life over my own circumstances! Through the grace of God, I was preaching life into my own situation without knowing it! Who would have known that by preaching faith and life to others, I was also speaking faith and life over myself?!!! Only God!!!!

Our daughter Lachelle is a spoken word poet. She acquired this skill during Middle School and perfected it throughout high school. As a preacher and pastor, I use words all the time but Lachelle is a speaker. In fact, she is a better speaker than I am. She knows the power of written words and the liberation that comes from speaking those words the right way. Don't miss what I just wrote: written words have power but words spoken the right way bring freedom. This is why speaking God's Word into your season of depression is so important. It is okay to speak to God about your depression, but you must also speak to your depression about God. We often refer to the spirit of depression as the "state of depression." Remember, depression is not a state – it is a spirit. Since depression is a spirit, you must speak the Word of God over it. The God who began a good work in you is still working on you and through you. You are His work in progress and He still has you under construction. Let God's Word complete God's work in you. Consider what Paul says in Colossians 3:16:

[16] *Let the word of Christ dwell in you richly in all wisdom; teaching and admonishing one another in psalms and hymns and spiritual songs, singing with grace in your hearts to the Lord.*

You must work with God to turn your sadness into gladness. Start singing songs of praise, hymns, and speaking God's Word into your depression. This will not be easy but stay faithful to the process! God does not do for you what you don't work for yourself. You have a part to play in the process! Remember, faith without work is dead or non-productive. Your part is to SPEAK God's Word to your depression each and every day! Read His Word, Write His Word, Sing His Word, and Speak His Word! Your deliverance from depression may not happen overnight but it will happen. My deliverance from depression came over a five year period after faithfully speaking God's Word into others. I should tell you that five is the number of grace. Each day I am alive, I am eternally thankful for His Amazing Grace!! By grace, God used my calling to the pulpit to pull me from the pit of depression.

Divine Declaration: *Lord, I decree and declare that as I endure the process of coming into Your Light, the shadow of depression will give way to the light of your joy!*

“For His anger endureth but a moment but in His favor is life, weeping endureth for a night but joy cometh in the morning.”
- Psalm 30:5

Chapter Six:

The Next Season

***

It’s not easy seeing the picture when you are the frame. As the frame, I could not see that God was using depression to create a better picture for my life. It has often been said that after every dark cloud there is a silver lining. Now that I am in the next season of my life, I have discovered that damp, cold and dreary nights are followed by the brightness of the shining sun. My season of depression was a dark period in my life that brought much sadness, suffering, and sorrow. In its path, I’ve learned how to live, love, and let God. God never promised an easy life; He promised the power to endure. We overcome depression by learning how to live one day at a time. Each day I survived depression was a day closer to my deliverance. Overcoming depression is not easy because if you are not careful, you can easily slip back into it. Overcoming depression is as much progressive as it is productive. Each day, I fight and press forward. Regardless of whether it is in my personal, private, or professional life, I chose not to allow the situations and storms of this life to depress me.

Each individual (whether depressed or not), must decide not to allow the vicissitudes of life to depress them. This is a daily decision that we must make for the rest of our lives. The key to making this decision is to never give up on yourself or God. Don't give up in the fight! If you don't give up, you (like me) will discover that life is filled with periods and commas.

In the English language, a period is a punctuation mark that represents a closing or an ending. On the other hand, a comma is a punctuation mark that represents a continuation after a pause. God works through periods (closings) and pauses (continuations). Depression was supposed to be a closing in my life because it was meant to destroy me. Had I given up on God (or on myself), my depression would have fulfilled its purpose. By grace, God flips the script and takes what the enemy means for a closing and turns it into a continuation. Calvary teaches us that God transforms periods into pauses. At Calvary, what was supposed to be a period (Christ's death) becomes a pause by His resurrection. By the power of the resurrection, God transforms periods into pauses and turns closings into continuations. Because God transformed my depression (period) into a pause, I experience the joy and satisfaction of a newfound inner peace.

To Choose or Not to Choose

Overcoming depression is a challenge but staying depressed is a choice. Many people are depressed because they choose to stay in that condition. Although it seemed as if my depression had come from nowhere, once I identified the problem I still had to make a choice. I do not claim to be a clinical counselor or a psychologist. However, Choice Theory and Reality Therapy identifies depression as a means of grappling with the area that exists between what we want and what we have. According to this theory and therapy, depression does not come from having what we want; depression comes when we stop wanting what we have. Consequently, Choice Theory and Reality Therapy do not necessarily view depression as a bad thing or as not being able to be overcome when it occurs. The key to overcoming depression is by choosing not to stay depressed and changing how you think and act. In other words, you must think the right way, make the right choices, and do the right things.

My depression experience taught me that depression produces four unique elements. Knowing these elements can help you overcome the darkness of depression. These four elements are outlined in the following sections that I call: I ACHE. (Anger, Control, Help, Excuses)

I was Angry

Being depressed angered me. I was angry with God and I was angry with myself and others. If not confronted, anger becomes bitterness that turns to hate. Unaddressed anger is not only dangerous, it is deadly. Thankfully, I came to realize that staying angry and depressed longer than I needed to was way too dangerous. I reasoned that it would be much better if I were not angry and depressed. In my depression, I took my anger out on others which only alienated people and made matters worse. I was falling into the trap of allowing anger to destroy my relationships and my life and although anger could be used as positive reinforcement, it was also destructive. I could not allow myself to stay depressed even though I felt as it was a safe alternative to moving forward and dealing with the unknown. Sometimes dealing with the unknown is a necessary means for survival.

I wanted Control

When I was depressed, I knew I had lost control of my everyday life and was losing more control with each passing day. However, I still forced myself to believe I had some measure of control over my condition. This was a complete lie. Depression is a very deceptive force. Depression makes you feel safe by keeping you from living a fulfilling life. It paralyzes you in time and affects those around you. When my staff or others saw I was in a dark place or sensed a shift in mood or personality, it made them feel uncomfortable. I wanted them to think that I was in control even though I knew I wasn't. Many times, the only thing they would do was avoid doing something that would make me upset, sad, or angry (agitate my depression). They knew that if I was angry or upset, I would take my anger out on them. Even when my life was out of control, depression had me believing I was still in control. That false sense of control came with a great price – I continued to suffer in silence. I can tell you from experience that depressed people don't like being depressed. Take my word for it, I'm a true witness!

I needed Help

I needed help. Help was not something I wanted from God, help was something I needed from Him. I realized there was no way I would be able to overcome the spirit of depression alone. What started as a problem was now a spiritual stronghold. I was mentally, emotionally, and spiritually bound. I was numb to life, indifferent to living, and everything around me was veiled in a fog of confusion.

When diagnosed, depression can draw a certain amount of help from family, friends, physicians, counselors, support groups, loved ones, therapists, etc. As a point of information, some people experiencing depression will require long term help while others will require short term help. In any event, the longer the period of depression, the more resources you will need for continual help or assistance. Unfortunately, your supporters can eventually grow weary in long term help because they want to move on with their lives. This can cause the depression itself to be seen as a burden and the individual as a bother. This is very disheartening and can be very dangerous. It is also why many people struggling with depression refuse to seek or ask for help. Nobody wants to feel as if they are a bother or a burden to others.

During my season of depression, if someone had asked "What's wrong?" I would have instinctively replied, "Nothing." This was not because I had resorted to being a serial liar. It was simply because I did not want others to consider me as a burden or a bother. If you are like me, I am sure you have struggled with this during your depression also. Like so many others who have struggled with depression – although I knew something was wrong, I was willing to be untruthful with myself and others.

Depression stands between you and God and must be brought into the Light. Trust me, it is not worth hiding your depression from others. We all need help sometimes and there is no shame in asking for it. Help is HEALTHY so asking for help is okay! God uses others to help us and He uses us to help others. Asking for help is not weakness but strength. It takes profound courage and great strength to admit you need help and ask for it. I have learned that God will never dismiss a sincere cry for help. He may not be there when you WANT Him, but He is always there when you NEED Him!

I was making Excuses

An excuse is an attempt to lessen the blame for a fault or offense or an attempt to defend or justify it. When I was a freshman at Florida Memorial College in Miami, Florida, I was introduced to the following anonymous quote about excuses: "*Excuses are the tools of the incompetent which build monuments of nothing and those who specialize in them seldom accomplish anything.*" I learned very quickly that Florida Memorial was a place where excuses were not welcomed. These words have always had a sense of strong importance and profound intellect with me and I never forgot them.

Drawing from my earlier years at Florida Memorial, I knew I could not make excuses for my depression. If I chose to stay depressed, I would have been making excuses for not taking responsibility of my life. If I were not careful, my depression would have become an avenue for dependence. Depression had made it very difficult for me to get up, get out and about, get dressed, go to work, and/or face my problems. Ironically, it was only when I began to do these and other simple tasks that I began to regain control of my life and overcome depression. The Choice Theory principle simply stated that if I were to overcome depression, I had to take direct action.

When I was depressed, my thinking had been compromised. Depression had given me very little control over my thought process and little (if any) control over my emotions. All I could do was try to get out of the shadow of depression and move to a place of mental clarity. Only then would I be in a position to gain control of my decisions and my actions. Some days it took everything I had just to get out of bed.

It took five years for me to overcome the spirit of depression. I have sinse learned that thoughts, feelings, and actions are all connected and sometimes we must form good habits before we can develop positive feelings about the things we do. Although this process was very slow, it was effective. Trying to "pull yourself together" or "snap out of it" is a counterproductive approach to solving the problem. When depressed, you cannot just "pull yourself together" or "snap out of it" because you are fighting against a spirit that keeps you in bondage. You must strategically fight this spirit to survive. For me, fighting this spirit also involved strategically changing my thoughts and behavior to form good habits. Although it was hard work, I am grateful for the long term effects they provided.

The "I" Factor

My father once told me that being a man means taking responsibility for your responsibilities. If you noticed, each of the four sections above began with the word "I." This is because overcoming depression is going to be ultimately up to you. Just as I could not blame anyone for my depression, I could not expect anyone to rescue me from it. Since faith without works is dead, faith alone would not be enough – I had to make a commitment to do the hard work. Having faith in God is one thing, but acting on that faith is another. God enabled me to overcome depression because of my faith in Him and my commitment to doing the work that was required. If you are going to overcome your depression, you cannot keep running from it. You must use all your strength to take responsibility for your life. Like my father said, we must take responsibility for our responsibilities.

In God's Favor is Life

God is Love and God is Light. My season of depression was a night time experience. Regardless of how dark, dreary, and dismal my depression, it did not stop the exciting and effervescent joy that came with the dawn of a new day in my life. Overcoming depression ushered a new chapter in my life which brought many new encounters and experiences. Overcoming depression showed me that in God's favor is Life. God wants you to live but you must decide to live. Living is a decision you must make. Like David, I am a witness that weeping lasts only for a night but true joy comes in the morning! Although overcoming depression was not easy, the joy and peace that I gained from the experience has made it all worth the while.

Psalm 30:5 lets us know God's anger is momentary. I am certain that many times during my season of depression I gave God reasons to be angry with me. However, God's anger is a different type of anger - it's momentary. God is not angry with you and He is not angry that you are depressed. God proves this by tempering your season of weeping to be only for a night. Depression lasts as long as you stay in its shadow. Come into the Light! The Light of God's love still shines in your life and He wants you to have true joy. Let the Light of God's love become your morning joy!

Divine Declaration: *Lord, I decree and declare that my next chapter will bring honor and glory to Your Name and that in spite of my season of depression, I will bless Your Name!*

"To appoint unto them that mourn in Zion, to give unto them beauty for ashes, the oil of joy for mourning, the garment of praise for the spirit of heaviness; that they might be called trees of righteousness, the planting of the LORD, that he might be glorified."
– Isaiah 61:3

Chapter Seven:

The Other Side of Depression

***

The Prophet Elijah suffered from severe depression. After Jezebel puts a hit on his life, he ran into the wilderness and asks God to take his life *(I Kings 18)*. For the record, Elijah really didn't want to die. Jezebel already had a hit on his life so if he really wanted to die, she would have answered that prayer for him! Elijah had just experienced the glory of God on Mt. Carmel *(I Kings 17)* and now he was running for his life in the wilderness *(I Kings 18)*. Like many, Elijah had been attacked by the spirit of depression through hurt and was in a place of dejection, destitution, and despair. It is interesting that being a prophet did not stop Elijah from being depressed. As prophet, Elijah carried a mantle everywhere he went. The mantle represents God's anointing and as you carry the mantle, you must understand you are more susceptible to depression. Elijah's mantle reflected seasons of drought, fire, and rain. God has given each of us a mantle from which we experience drought (poverty), fire (purification), and rain (prosperity). These are the seasons of God's mantle for your life.

Depression changed me forever. Now that I am on the other side of it, I am a totally different person and I see things in a totally different way. My wife Michelle lives by the creed, "Everything has a home." I did not understand what she meant by this initially, but I've come to understand it over time. When I first met her, I thought she may have had some sort of disorder. Unlike me who just puts things down and (may or may not) come back to them later, she instinctively finds a place for everything. I've since realized that maybe I was the one with the disorder. A home is a "place to belong." When things don't have a home, they have no purpose or place to belong. Consequently, items can pile up any and everywhere. Eventually, everything around us becomes cluttered, confusing, and chaotic. In our home, my wife eventually finds a home for everything. Everything has to have a place to belong.

I have learned that depression has a home, a place to belong, a purpose in my life. Although I no longer suffer from depression, I still struggle against it. Frederick Douglass said, "Where there is no struggle, there is no progress." You cannot have a personal story without a painful struggle. My painful struggle with the spirit of depression is also my personal story. Through the struggle, I have made great progress and my life will forever be changed by my experience. Depression was a test that has become my testimony. Even though I am on the other side of depression, there are still times I feel myself going down that slippery slope. My experience helps me identify the symptoms of depression so I can fight against that spirit before it becomes a stronghold in my life. Because of this, everything about me is different – I think differently, I act differently, I live differently, I am different. Not only am I a different person, but I now live in a different place.

When you are depressed, you become susceptible to at least two (2) other types of spiritual attacks: the spirit of fear and the spirit of suicide. Consider what the Apostle Paul has to say about the spirit of fear in II Timothy 1:7:

> [7] *For God hath not given us the spirit of fear; but of power, and of love, and of a sound mind.*

Notice that fear is called as a spirit. A spirit cannot be defeated by natural means. In spiritual warfare, you cannot use natural methodologies to defeat a spiritual force. Fear brings bondage, despair, and torment. It paralyzes us while preventing us from moving forward in the process. The only way we can overcome the spirit of fear is with God's power, God's love, and God's way of thinking (sound mind). Fear, suicide, and depression cause us to think contrary to the Word of God. Don't lose your mind to the enemy! These spirits often make us feel as if we are helpless and hopeless. Feelings of helplessness and hopelessness are tools from the enemy. With God, we are never helpless or hopeless.

The spirit of fear and the spirit of suicide are closely related. In addition to what the Apostle Paul says about the spirit of fear in II Timothy 1:7; consider what Jesus says about the spirit of death and destruction (suicide) in John 10:10:

> ***The thief cometh*** *not, but for to steal, and to* ***kill****, and to* ***destroy****: I am come that they might have life, and that they might have it more abundantly.*

The spirit of suicide is a thief! This spirit has taken the lives of countless people. So many families today are shattered trying to deal with the aftermath of suicide. The person who committed suicide is gone, joy is gone, and the lives of those left behind are destroyed. Jesus plainly states that this spirit is out to steal your joy and destroy your desire for living. This spirit's method of operation is stealing, killing, and destroying. Sometimes, that destruction can come from your own hands. In addition to being a spirit of destruction, suicide is a trick from the enemy! God's desire for you is to live in awareness, assurance, and abundance. Take it from me, when you are gripped by fear and feel as if you are in a hopeless situation, thoughts of suicide become more appealing. It's not so much that you want to stop living, you just want to stop living in pain, with pain, and through pain. The constant and endless cycle of pain that comes from depression can be overwhelming. Whether the pain be physical, emotional, mental, or spiritual, it can wreak havoc in your life. Many (if not most) people who commit suicide just want to escape the pain. It is only by the grace of God that I did not give in to the temptation of suicide. There were many days where I felt like taking a few extra pills or a long drive over a short bridge. I know what it is to have a tidal wave of suicidal thoughts invade your mind. If you are facing thoughts of suicide, you are not crazy. You are under a spirit attack from the enemy. I know the pain you are facing and what it is to be in so much pain that you feel like giving up. During my season of depression, I just wanted the pain to go away.

Since my years of depression, God has relocated me from my former pastoral assignment. On October 3, 2015, I was confirmed as the Senior Pastor of the Shiloh Baptist Church in York, Pennsylvania. My 20 years of service as Senior Pastor of the St. Andrew Missionary Baptist Church in Miami, Florida and my 7 years of service as its youth minister was a proving ground for me. I was healed from the spirit of depression in 2008 and afterwards, served another 7 years as Senior Pastor of St. Andrew Baptist Church. During that time, the church still experienced ministry challenges. The difference is that I now saw things differently. I now understand that if I don't change how I see challenges, I could just as easily slip back into depression.

Living on the other side of depression is my daily struggle to survive. As I stated earlier, wounds heal but scars last a life time. Struggling to survive is the scar that reminds me each day not to allow myself to return to that shadow. Each day, I must decide to focus on thinking in a way that will produce victory in my life and not defeat. In addition to my normal pastoral duties, I must seek the positive even in the most negative of situations. Like me, you will be challenged in your life after depression. Challenges are a necessary part of life; they will either build you up or break you down. It all depends on your perception!!

The Beauty for Ashes

Isaiah 61 is a beautiful illustration of God's power to restore, revive, and renew. God is a God of restoration and He is able to give you double for your trouble – just ask Job (Job 42:10)!!! In Hebrew culture, ashes represent mourning, grief, and sorrow. It was also related to repentance and turning back to God. You don't have to live in constant sorrow and perpetual pain. Don't allow the enemy to make you think your life is over and nothing more can be done to change your situation. God specializes in things that seem impossible and He can do what no other power can do! God has a way of using our grief's and sorrows to produce beauty within. He uses the worst situations to bring out the best in us. In other words, what was sorrowful for us will be a beautiful story for others to read. Your story is still being written by the Author and Finisher of your Faith. God uses your story to bring salvation to the lives of others. It is through our grief and sorrows that God brings others to Him. God is using your depression as a testimony of faith and a thing of beauty. Only God can transform the ashes of your depression into the beauty of His grace. God wants to exchange your ashes for His beauty. You might ask, "How does God take the ashes of something as ugly as depression and make it beautiful?" **He gets in the depression with us – that's Grace!**

The Oil of Joy

God does not give us the oil of joy, He produces it. Oil cannot be produced without immense heat and intense pressure. In life, our tests, trials, and tribulations places us under immense heat and intense pressure. It is through the process of going through that the oil of joy is produced in us. Oil represents the presence of God's Spirit and anointing. I came out of my season of depression in 2008. On December 13 of that same year, I met the woman who would later marry. Through the intensity of my depression, God produced the oil of joy in my life in more ways than one.

Understand that God uses your appointment with depression to anoint you with the oil of joy. I say this because I have found true joy on the other side of depression! I now know that what I thought was joy was really happiness. Happiness is a feeling, but joy is faith! Joy is Christ Personified! Depression showed me that true joy is having faith that God is present in every situation. True joy is a testimony of faith. I'm not joyful because I feel God, I'm joyful because I know God. In the words of Job 11:25,

> *25For I know that my redeemer liveth, and that he shall stand at the latter day upon the earth:*

Job's story shows us that he could relate to depression. He was a man who lost everything but in the end, God gave him twice as much as he lost (Job 42:10). Like Job's story, my depression reconfirmed my belief that God lives. I also learned that when the dust settles, God is the last one standing.

Depression tests our faith. My season of depression was a test of my faith. Knowing God lives increases my faith in Him. In my season of depression, my faith was revived, renewed, and refined.

The Garment of Praise

Our daughter Shanika has a beautiful singing voice. She literally sings without any effort and her voice can bring healing to those who are broken. I wish I had a voice to sing like that! If she ever decided to record, I am certain she would be a very successful artist. Unlike Shanika's singing ability, praise takes great effort when you are depressed. When the spirit of depression attacks the soul, praising God becomes very difficult. I know from personal experience that praising God when you are depressed is a struggle. When Isaiah talks about the garment of praise, he suggests that we wear our praise like a garment. In addition to being a garment, our praise is like a magnifying glass. Praise enlarges the object of our attention or focus. When God is our focus, our praise makes Him bigger to others. This is why in Psalm 34:3-4, David declares:

> *'Magnify the Lord with me, and let us exalt his name together. I sought the Lord, and he heard me, and delivered me from all my fears'*

If you are waiting for your depression to pass before you praise God, you are making a huge mistake. Throughout the Bible, praise is used as weapon to solve problems. If you are going to overcome the spirit of depression, you must put on the garment of praise and make God your focus. Right where you are, Praise God and hold on! When you praise God, you make God bigger than your depression. Right where you are, Praise God and don't give up! When you praise God, you make Him the Solution to every problem. Right where you are, just Praise God! Introduce your problem to the power of your praise!

In Isaiah 61, God promises those who come to Him 'the garment of praise for the spirit of heaviness.' When you praise God in your heaviness, He gives you a change of clothes. Take off the grave clothes of depression and put on the garments of praise! When you put on the garments of praise, you will receive new hope and eternal joy. In your praise, you are reminded that our God is bigger than depression. When you make God bigger than depression, depression will no longer have a foothold in your life. God is worthy of your praise because of His Might, His Mercy, His Majesty, and His Miracles. Surviving depression is a miracle and you are a living, walking, talking, miracle!!! Remove the spirit of heaviness (depression) and put on the garment of praise!

The Spirit of Heaviness

Psalm 137:1-4 records the following:

By the rivers of Babylon, there we sat down, yea, we wept, when we remembered Zion.

[2] *We hanged our harps upon the willows in the midst thereof.*

[3] *For there they that carried us away captive required of us a song; and they that wasted us required of us mirth, saying, Sing us one of the songs of Zion.*

[4] *How shall we sing the LORD's song in a strange land?*

This Psalm outlines the depression God's people experienced as they entered Babylonian captivity. The people were depressed and singing God's song in a strange land was an insurmountable task under the existing conditions. The Bible calls depression the "spirit of heaviness." This is why I believe depression is a spiritual attack. When you are in a season of depression, you are not crazy, insane, or losing your mind. You are simply under a spiritual attack from the enemy.

The spirit of depression is very subtle. It starts out as an area (or areas) of minute cares or minor concerns. Over time, what starts out as a small bother grows into a great burden. Life eventually becomes a ball of confusion. Everything about us, (actions, thoughts, words, etc.) begin to reflect a troubled heart, a heavy spirit, and a burdened mind. The assignment of the spirit of depression is to <u>distort</u> your mind, distract your heart, and disturb your spirit. Depression keeps our heads down so we can't look up. Listen to the words of David in Psalm 121:1:

> ***I will lift up*** *mine* ***eyes*** *unto the hills, from whence cometh my help. My help cometh from the LORD, which made heaven and earth.*

To look up, we must first lift our eyes. Depression wears you down to the point where you seem helpless and hopeless. I have discovered that the spirit of depression wants to replace God's presence in your life. It wants to make you feel as if God is not there. The only way we can overcome the spirit of depression is to be clothed with the garment of praise. When God inhabits your praise, He comes into the midst of your praise and works on your behalf! When you begin to praise God, His Spirit shows up and the spirit of depression must take a flight!

If you are under attack by the spirit of depression, there is only one thing you can do, need to do, and must do! In the midst of your heaviness, open your mouth, share your testimony, and bless God! Press through the weight of your heaviness (depression) to decree and declare God's goodness in this season of depression. Stir up your praise even when you don't feel like it. Depression does not want you to praise God and makes praising Him difficult. Your body may get tired, your mind may get confused, and your spirit may get worn but praise God anyhow! Overcoming the spirit of depression is a fight to survive. Sometimes we must be like David and encourage and/or will ourselves to praise God and declare His Word even when we don't feel like it.

Don't miss this. Sometimes we must will ourselves to praise God even when we don't feel like it! You must will yourself to take off the spirit of depression and put on the garment of praise! Instead of focusing on the magnitude of your problems, focus on the magnificence of your God! Praise God and magnify Him in the face of your depression! Don't let the spirit of depression get the best of your praise!

The Trees of Righteousness

It is interesting that God compares those who have come through depression as trees. Trees are common throughout the world and can be found in every climate, country, culture, city, and community. Trees are strong, sturdy, and secure and reflect change. Each year, trees grow, change, or shed their leaves to show the changing of seasons. In addition, trees provide shade from the sun, food for the hungry, shelter for the weary, and beauty for the world. At some point in life, we have all had some dealings with trees. As a child, I remember climbing trees, swinging and jumping from trees, and hiding behind trees. Trees also help cleanse the atmosphere by converting carbon-dioxide to oxygen so we can breathe.

In Psalm 1:3, David says the following:

> *He will be like a tree planted by the streams of water, that brings forth its fruit in its season, whose leaf also does not wither. Whatever he does shall prosper.*

Whereas depression symbolizes death, trees symbolize life and reflect seasons of faith, fruitfulness, and favor. God wants us to have faith, be fruitful, and experience His favor. Favor says that whatever we do will surely prosper.

As trees of righteousness, God plants us in places where He intends for us to prosper. Notice how God prospers us after we have been planted. After being planted, it takes time to prosper. In David's narrative, the streams of water, fruitfulness, and green leaves show that God still favors us through tough times. Although seasons of depression may be tough, they do not stop God from prospering you. God's prosperity is bigger than your depression. Let me encourage you: depression is not a stumbling block, depression is a stepping stone to the next level. You are a tree of righteousness because God has planted you where you are for such a time as this!

Planting God's Glory

It's interesting to note that Isaiah 61 begins with words that personally affirms God's Spirit and anointing upon the individual. There is a powerful connection between God, the anointing, and the individual. In the Bible, the word anointing means to make grow or become fat. When we are anointed, yokes are destroyed because we are made to grow and become fat. For me, the ultimate purpose for depression was to grow in God's glory. Growing in God's glory requires that I plant God's glory in someone else. Now that I am on the other side of depression, I must share God's glory by planting it in others. I want to plant God's glory in you!

Not only must we be planted in God's glory, we must also plant God's glory in others. Planting God's glory means sharing your faith, your story, and your testimony with others. Your season of depression was designed to insert God's glory into your story. Without God's glory, your story is incomplete. God's glory is submerged in Scripture and is woven throughout every verse and story. God's glory underscores the grace of our salvation in Jesus Christ and is the ultimate goal of redemption.

What is God's glory? God's glory is the reflection of Himself in you. It is His perfected will and purpose in all things. God's glory is the manifestation of His inexhaustible beauty and supreme greatness in all things and that includes you! God's glory is the visible manifestation of his nature, attributes, and character. God's glory is God looking at Himself in the mirror of His divine love and holiness. It is God seeing Himself in you and manifesting Himself within you and the rest of His creation.

According to Psalm 19:1, the heavens tell of God's glory. What this means is that God is speaking to us through nature. He speaks to us through everything He has created. The sun, the moon, the stars, the clouds, the galaxies, and the entire universe testify of God's glory. Animals, plants, insects, micro-organisms and all other life forms testify of God's glory. Depression keeps us from hearing and seeing God's glory. It blinds our eyes and deafens our ears to God's glory even when it is right in front of us.

We seek a Holy God who wants us to see His glory. Seeing God's glory makes it easier to serve Him. God is Holy and all creation testifies of His glory. I write this book to let you know that you were made for God's glory. Depression tried to destroy you but you survived. Just as I survived my journey from pulpit depression, you survived your journey from personal depression. I decree that today is your day of deliverance. You were made to survive the spirit of depression and live the life of an overcomer.

If you are reading this book, then you survived the very thing that was meant to destroy you. Your survival means that God is on your side and you are victorious. Depression could not defeat you, destroy you, or deceive you. You are still standing, you are still strong, and you are still surviving! Like me, you're a survivor! We have survived a tedious, tempestuous, and tiresome journey to freedom beyond depression. As a survivor you are alive, you are strong, and you are free. Never forget that you are now, and forever will be, a survivor of depression! Don't allow depression to bring you down to its level. God did not bring you out of depression for you to exist beyond it, He brought you out of depression to live above it!

Don't fool yourself, the spirit of depression is real and it is a powerful enemy. If you are like me, you might feel as if you are all alone in your fight. Hear me, you are never alone in the fight against depression. God is always with you and you must trust Him even when you cannot trace Him. As a matter of fact, you are in great company! In the Bible, Moses, Elijah, David, Jeremiah, Job, and even Jesus struggled with depression.

Depression is mental, physical, emotional, and spiritual. It is an endless feeling of hopelessness and despair in the world we live. Living in a world without hope only reflects hopelessness. Depression is the internal manifestation of loss and hopelessness. Hope in God will help us defeat depression. If we have hope, we can and will overcome depression. Through hope, we are able to see a bigger, better, and brighter future. Without hope, you will have no desire to live or move on. Be encouraged in your hope today! It is the Word of God that encourages your heart and gives you that hope.

Abraham Lincoln was one of the greatest presidents in U.S. history. Before becoming the 16th President of the United States, he experienced many setbacks and defeats. Some of these defeats included him losing his job, being defeated for state legislature, a failed business, the death of his fiancé, a nervous breakdown, defeated for speaker, defeated for congressional nomination and losing re-nomination (after winning in 1846), rejected for land officer, twice defeated for U.S. Senate, and defeated in a bid for Vice President nomination. All this happened before he became President. With as many defeats as Lincoln experienced, it's a miracle that he remained persistent enough to keep striving for success. I don't know of too many people who would not have gone on to suffer from a serious case of chronic depression.

Throughout his adulthood, it is recorded that Lincoln battled suicide and struggled with depression. For his own protection (and others), he would avoid carrying weapons out of fear of hurting himself or someone else. It was during these times that Lincoln found strength in God's Word to fight depression. Lincoln is a shining example of how the Word of God gives you complete and total victory over the spirit of depression. Notice again that I wrote the "spirit of depression." Remember, depression is a Spirit and can only be overcome by the Word of God.

Overcoming depression is a fight to survive. You must fight that fight with the Word of God. In addition, you must also speak scriptures into your spirit that suppresses depression and defeats hopelessness. If you are reading this book, you still have hope in what might appear to be a hopeless situation. However, your hope cannot be found in houses and land, riches and wealth, or in people. Your hope can only be found in Christ (the Solid Rock) and His Word. In the profound words of Edward Mote:

My hope is built on nothing less
Than Jesus' blood and righteousness;
I dare not trust the sweetest frame,
But wholly lean on Jesus' name.
On Christ, the solid Rock, I stand;
All other ground is sinking sand.

Overcoming the spirit of depression requires that we plow in hope. In life, plowing represents our perseverance, purpose, and promotion. If we are to see the rewards of plowing, we must *push* the plow, *break* the ground, and *plant* the seed. In ancient Israel, those who plowed the land would follow this pattern each day and every day. Whether the day was sunny, rainy, warm, cold, hot, windy, or dry – the process remained the same: *push* the plow, *break* the ground, and *plant* the seed. Regardless of how those who plowed the field felt – it was the same: *push* the plow, *break* the ground, and *plant* the seed. In I Corinthians 9:10, Paul writes about this when he discusses plowing in hope. Each day we plow in the hope of a better tomorrow. However, we will never reap the harvest of the field if we fail to plow the ground or plant the seed.

In God's Word, we find the hope we need to survive life's sinking sands and slippery slopes. That Hope is Jesus Christ. Christ is God's

Hope in troubled times. He is the Hope who motivates, encourages, and keeps us moving forward. In my season of depression, I rediscovered Jesus Christ. In doing so, I discovered that He is God's Eternal Hope of salvation. If you are struggling with depression in this season of your life, only Christ can produce faith, promote love, and propel you to victory over depression! God wants you to have an expected end! Consider Jeremiah 29:11:

> [11] *For I know the thoughts that I think toward you, saith the LORD, thoughts of peace, and not of evil, to give you an expected end.*

God has you on His mind and He wants to give you an expected end filled with JOY, HOPE, PEACE, and VICTORY! Allow God to finish your story and give you His expected end! Trust me when I speak into your life that you are not alone in this fight. You are important to God and you have value. God can and will help you overcome the spirit of depression. In your fight to overcome depression, use the following scriptures to combat the spirit of depression and build your faith. By building your faith, you will increase your hope, and cultivate trust in God. Speak these Scriptures and think on them to become victorious against the spirit of depression. Build your faith, increase your hope, and cultivate trust in God! Trust God to allow His Word to renew your spirit and restore your joy! Allow God's hope to flow though you to reach others who are depressed. Remember, God has provided for you, protected you, and prospered you for such a time as this. Prosper where you are planted and God will do the rest! Trees don't move on their own accord. They stand strong and weather the storms until they are moved. Stand strong and let God use your depression as a means to prosper you and promote you into your new season. Stand firm on God's promises! The promises of God are sure, safe, and satisfying! You don't have resort back into the abyss of depression and you don't have to feel that you are struggling alone. God is with you and He has given you His Word as a witness to His purpose and promises for your life. God has promised that you can and will make it. Hold on to the promises of God! He has promised that you will be the lender and not the borrower, you will be the head and not the tail, you will be above and not beneath, and you shall live and not die (Deuteronomy 28:13; Psalm 118:17)!!

Divine Declaration: *Lord, as I live on the other side of depression, I decree and declare through Your Name I will never be bound again by the spirit of depression!*

OVERCOMING THE SPIRIT OF DEPRESSION WITH THE WORD OF GOD

Deuteronomy 31:8

And the LORD, He it is that doth go before thee; He will be with thee, He will not fail thee, neither forsake thee: fear not, neither be dismayed.

Deuteronomy 33:27

The eternal God is thy refuge, and underneath are the everlasting arms: and He shall thrust out the enemy from before thee; and shall say, Destroy them.

2 Samuel 22:17-22

He sent from above, He took me; He drew me out of many waters; (18) He delivered me from my strong enemy, and from them that hated me: for they were too strong for me. (19) They prevented me in the day of my calamity: but the LORD was my stay. (20) He brought me forth also into a large place: He delivered me, because He delighted in me. (21) The LORD rewarded me according to my righteousness: according to the cleanness of my hands hath he recompensed me. (22) For I have kept the ways of the LORD, and have not wickedly departed from my God.

2 Samuel 22:29

For thou art my lamp, O LORD: and the LORD will lighten my darkness.

Ecclesiastes 9:4

For to him that is joined to all the living there is hope: for a living dog is better than a dead lion.

Psalms 9:9

The LORD also will be a refuge for the oppressed, a refuge in times of trouble.

Psalm 27:14

Wait on the LORD: be of good courage, and He shall strengthen thine heart: wait, I say, on the LORD.

Psalm 31:22-24

For I said in my haste, I am cut off from before thine eyes: nevertheless thou heardest the voice of my supplications when I cried unto thee. (23)O love the LORD, all ye his saints: for the LORD preserveth the faithful, and plentifully rewardeth the proud doer. (24)Be of good courage, and he shall strengthen your heart, all ye that hope in the LORD.

Psalm 34:18, 19

The LORD is nigh unto them that are of a broken heart; and saveth such as be of a contrite spirit. (19) Many are the afflictions of the righteous: but the LORD delivereth him out of them all.

Psalm 37:23-24

The steps of a good man are ordered by the LORD: and he delighteth in his way. (24) Though he fall, he shall not be utterly cast down: for the LORD upholdeth him with his hand.

Psalm 43:5

Why art thou cast down, O my soul? and why art thou disquieted within me? hope in God: for I shall yet praise him, who is the health of my countenance, and my God.

Psalm 55:22

Cast thy burden upon the LORD, and he shall sustain thee: he shall never suffer the righteous to be moved.

Psalm 62:5

My soul, wait thou only upon God; for my expectation is from him.

Psalm 126:5

They that sow in tears shall reap in joy.

Psalm 143:7-8

Hear me speedily, O LORD: my spirit faileth: hide not thy face from me, lest I be like unto them that go down into the pit.(8) Cause me to hear thy lovingkindness in the morning; for in thee do I trust: cause me to know the way wherein I should walk; for I lift up my soul unto thee.

Psalm 145:14

The LORD upholdeth all that fall, and raiseth up all those that be bowed down.

Psalm 147:3

He healeth the broken in heart, and bindeth up their wounds.

Proverbs 12:25

Heaviness in the heart of man maketh it stoop: but a good word maketh it glad.

Isaiah 26:3-4

Thou wilt keep him in perfect peace, whose mind is stayed on thee: because he trusteth in thee. (4) Trust ye in the LORD ever: for in the LORD JEHOVAH is everlasting strength: Thou wilt keep him in perfect peace, whose mind is stayed on Thee: because he trusts in Thee. Trust ye in the LORD for ever: for in the LORD JEHOVAH is everlasting strength.

Isaiah 35:10

– And the ransomed of the LORD shall return, and come to Zion with songs and everlasting joy upon their heads: they shall obtain joy and gladness, and sorrow and sighing shall flee away.

Isaiah 40:31

But they that wait upon the LORD shall renew their strength; they shall mount up with wings as eagles; they shall run, and not be weary; and they shall walk, and not faint.

Isaiah 53:4

Surely he hath borne our griefs, and carried our sorrows: yet we did esteem him stricken, smitten of God, and afflicted.

Matthew 11:28-30

Come unto me, all ye that labour and are heavy laden, and I will give you rest. (29)Take my yoke upon you, and learn of me; for I am meek and lowly in heart: and ye shall find rest unto your souls. (30) For my yoke is easy, and my burden is light.

Mark 9:23

Jesus said unto him, If thou canst believe, all things are possible to him that believeth.

Romans 4:18-22

Who against hope believed in hope, that he might become the father of many nations, according to that which was spoken, So shall thy seed be. (19) And being not weak in faith, he considered not his own body now dead, when he was about an hundred years old, neither yet the deadness of Sarah's womb(20) He staggered not at the promise of God through unbelief; but was strong in faith, giving glory to God; (21) And being fully persuaded that, what he had promised, he was able also to perform. (22) And therefore it was imputed to him for righteousness. Who against hope believed in hope, that he might become the father of many nations, according to that which was spoken, so shall they seed be.

Romans 15:13

Now the God of hope fill you with all joy and peace in believing, that ye may abound in hope, through the power of the Holy Ghost.

II Corinthians 7:6-7

Nevertheless God, that comforteth those that are cast down, comforted us by the coming of Titus; (7) And not by his coming only, but by the consolation wherewith he was comforted in you, when he told us your earnest desire, your mourning, your fervent mind toward me; so that I rejoiced the more.

Philippians 4:6-7

Be careful for nothing; but in everything by prayer and supplication with thanksgiving let your requests be made known unto God. (7) And the peace of God, which passeth all understanding, shall keep your hearts and minds through Christ Jesus.

James 4:8

Draw nigh to God, and he will draw nigh to you. Cleanse your hands, ye sinners; and purify your hearts, ye double minded.

James 4:10

Humble yourselves in the sight of the Lord, and He shall lift you up.

2 Peter 2:9

The Lord knoweth how to deliver the godly out of temptations, and to reserve the unjust unto the Day of Judgment to be punished:

1 Peter 4:12

Beloved, think it not strange concerning the fiery trial which is to try you, as though some strange thing happened unto you: But rejoice, inasmuch as ye are partakers of Christ's sufferings; that, when His glory shall be revealed, ye may be glad also with exceeding joy.

1 Peter 5:7

Casting all your care upon Him; for He careth for you.

VERCOMING THE SPIRIT OF DEPRESSION THROUGH HELPFUL ASSISTANCE

1. *A Place Called Hope*
   www.aplaceofhopechristiancounseling.com/treatment-programs/depression-anxiety

2. *Christian Counselors*
   www.betterhelp.com

3. *Emerge Counseling Services*
   www.emerge.org/clinicians

4. *Focus on the Family*
   http://www.focusonthefamily.com/lifechallenges/emotional-health

5. *Lives Transforming*
   https://www.livestransforming.com/renewing-the-mind/

6. *Mercy Multiplied*
   www.mercymultiplied.com/depression

7. *Gateway Counselling*
   https://gatewaycounseling.com/depression-anxiety/

8. *This Way Up*
   https://thiswayup.org.au/how-do-you-feel/sad/

34059319R00067

Made in the USA
Columbia, SC
13 November 2018